Rediscoveries in Children's Literature

CHILDREN'S LITERATURE AND CULTURE
VOLUME 2
GARLAND REFERENCE LIBRARY OF SOCIAL SCIENCE
VOLUME 862

Children's Literature and Culture

Jack Zipes, *General Editor*

Children's Literature
Comes of Age
Toward a New Aesthetic
by Maria Nikolajeva

Rediscoveries in
Children's Literature
by Suzanne Rahn

Rediscoveries in Children's Literature

Suzanne Rahn

Garland Publishing, Inc.
New York and London
1995

Library of Congress Cataloging-in-Publication Data

Rahn, Suzanne.
    Rediscoveries in children's literature / Suzanne Rahn.
        p.   cm. — (Garland reference library of social science ; v. 862. Children's
    literature and culture ; v. 2)
        Includes bibliographical references and index.
        ISBN 0-8153-0930-9
        1. Children's literature, American—History and criticism. 2. Children's lit-
    erature, English—History and criticism. 3. Lagerlöf, Selma, 1858–1940. Nils
    Holgerssons underbara resa. 4. Children—Books and reading. I. Title.
    II. Series: Garland reference library of social science ; v. 862. III. Series:
    Garland reference library of social science. Children's literature and
    culture ; v. 2.
    PS490.R25   1995   94-39594
                                                                          CIP

Cover illustration from *St. Nicholas Magazine* 9, 11 (September 1882):871.
Illustrations from *Made-to-Order Stories* by Dorothy Canfield, copyright 1925
by Harcourt Brace & Company and renewed 1953 by Dorothy Canfield Fisher,
copyright Jonathan Cape, reproduced by permission of the publishers.

Printed on acid-free, 250-year-life paper
Manufactured in the United States of America

For my mother
who read me good books

Contents

General Editor's Preface

Dedicated to furthering original research in children's literature and culture, the Children's Literature and Culture series will include monographs on individual authors and illustrators, historical examinations of different periods, literary analyses of genres, and comparative studies on literature and the mass media. The series is international in scope and is intended to encourage innovative research in children's literature with a focus on interdisciplinary methodology.

Children's literature and culture are understood in the broadest sense of the term "children" to encompass the period of childhood up through late adolescence. Due to the fact that the notion of childhood has changed so much since the origination of children's literature, this Garland series is particularly concerned with transformations in children's culture and how they have affected the representation and socialization of children. While the emphasis of the series is on children's literature, all types of studies that deal with children's radio, film, television, and art will be included in an endeavor to grasp the aesthetics and values of children's culture. Not only have there been momentous changes in children's culture in the last fifty years, but there have been radical shifts in the scholarship that deals with these changes. In this regard, the Children's Literature and Culture series wants to enhance research in this field and, at the same time, point to new directions that bring together the best scholarly work throughout the world.

Acknowledgments

This book and I owe a special debt to the encouragement of Geri DeLuca and Roni Natov, who published several of its chapters as articles in *The Lion and the Unicorn*; to Leonard Marcus, who deftly edited my first article for that journal; and to Jack Zipes, who found *Rediscoveries* its home.

I would like to thank Pacific Lutheran University, and especially Deans Janet Rasmussen and Paul Menzel, for their continuing support. A combined leave of absence and Regency Advancement Award from Pacific Lutheran enabled me to finish *Rediscoveries*.

Several friends have also given generously of their support and appreciation during the making of this book. I would especially like to thank Hamida Bosmajian, Sharon Jansen, Sherry Jones—and my husband John. And my mother, Mary Henry, who began it all.

Preface

As a child in the 1950s, I was dropped off at the library every Saturday, while my parents did their grocery shopping. The children's room was just to the right as you went in—a great, dim cave full of books. Its resources seemed inexhaustible. I could still lead you to the exact spot where the E. Nesbit fantasies were shelved, or the long line of Freddy the Pig books, or *Memoirs of a London Doll*, or the Doctor Dolittle books, or *The Little White Horse*, or *Peacock Pie*, or Laurence Housman's *A Doorway in Fairyland*, or the small, precious cache of historical novels by Geoffrey Trease, or Elizabeth Enright's *Spiderweb for Two*.

In my teens, I discovered that children's literature had a history. I read *A Critical History of Children's Literature* (by Cornelia Meigs and company) straight through. Here, enticingly described, were dozens of children's books I had never even heard of before. It was thanks to *A Critical History* that I sought out Jacob Abbott and Juliana Ewing and Charlotte Yonge and old, bound volumes of *St. Nicholas*. I also subscribed to *The Horn Book*, which told me that the flow of good children's books would never stop.

Twenty years later, children's literature had become a specialty for scholars and professors as well as children's librarians and elementary school teachers. Universities were offering courses, even graduate programs, in children's literature. New academic journals like *Children's Literature, The Lion and the Unicorn, Signal,* and *Children's Literature in Education* were publishing analyses of *Pinocchio* and *The Secret Garden*. I was compiling *Children's Literature: An Annotated Bibliography of the History and Criticism*—and not finding what I expected. For some authors, there might be a dozen critical essays—for others, nothing more than a memoir or an appreciation published in *The Horn Book* forty years ago.

With few exceptions, the kind of serious critical analysis I was looking for seemed limited to three categories of children's books: well-known, undisputed "classics"; works by a select handful of contemporary authors (the putative classics of the future); and formula fiction (such as Nancy Drew or the Bobbsey Twins). Books in the first two categories were accorded literary analysis from a variety of critical perspectives. Formula fiction, like popular fiction for adults, was scrutinized for what it could reveal about psychological needs, social attitudes, and cultural change.

The majority of what we had always simply called "good books"—books of high quality, distinct individuality, and staying power—had somehow fallen into the gap between. No one was writing about Geoffrey Trease or Laurence Housman or Juliana Ewing or Elizabeth Enright or Freddy the Pig. (No one was writing anything nice about Dr. Dolittle.) Was it simply a bias in favor of the contemporary? But even contemporary authors seemed to be chosen from a very restricted list.

In the process of becoming an academic field of study, children's literature had actually narrowed in scope. To some extent, this had happened by default. Many of the professors teaching (and later writing about) children's literature came to it with little background; assigned willy-nilly to teach a class, they were forced, at least temporarily, to rely on the "classics" everyone had heard of, and what they could pick up from awards, reviews, and textbooks for elementary school teachers about the contemporary scene. But to some extent, the narrowing was deliberate. In order to be accepted as a legitimate branch of literature with high standards of teaching and research, children's literature (some felt) must have an official canon—a list of literary "touchstones" with which no one could reasonably disagree. In 1980, the Children's Literature Association appointed a Canon Committee, and in 1985, the Committee presented a list of 63 books (or, in a few cases, pairs or series of books by the same author) which met their criteria of excellence and significance. This list became the basis of *Touchstones:*

Reflections on the Best in Children's Literature, edited by Perry Nodelman and published by the Association, a three-volume work in which each book was individually evaluated.

Although the intention of the Canon Committee was never to restrict the study of children's literature to the canon, its approach was essentially exclusive, even competitive. Only a few books were allowed to be "touchstones." (Most of Nodelman's introduction to Volume Three of *Touchstones* is an explanation of why so many fine authors were omitted.) Ironically, even as children's literature was acquiring a canon, canons themselves were coming increasingly under fire in the literary world at large, for this same tendency to exclude too much.

Meanwhile, since the 1970s, publishing houses have grown less inclined to preserve an extensive backlist of children's books. Only those books which consistently produce high profits are allowed to survive, and a number of "good books" have slipped quietly out of print. It is less likely than it used to be for a scholar or a teacher or a librarian—or a child—simply to come in contact with a book which is neither brand new nor extremely popular.

In contrast, what one might call the traditional approach to children's literature—the approach of my childhood library, *A Critical History*, and *The Horn Book*—was broadly inclusive. Even the Newbery and Caldecott Awards were soon expanded to include numerous Honor Books. There were lists and published series of "children's classics," but the term was used loosely; there was always room for more "good books." A typical example of this approach is *Realms of Gold in Children's Books*, published in 1929 by Bertha Mahony and Elinor Whitney. Despite the relatively low quality of children's literature during this decade, Mahony and Whitney have managed to cram every good book they can find between the covers of this large, fat, red volume. Even their title suggests limitless resources of good reading.

The effect of focusing all serious attention on a small number of books and authors is to diminish awareness of the richness and variety of children's literature. It becomes impossible to grasp the development of children's literature, or the context in which individual books were written. Ultimately, the study of children's literature is the poorer for ignoring so much fine material. And children are the poorer too, given fewer opportunities to hear of books that might enrich their lives.

Some book and journal editors have tried consciously to reverse the trend, encouraging contributors to seek out neglected books and authors. This book is also an attempt, not simply to "rediscover" a number of books that deserve to be better known, but to suggest how many "good books" are awaiting rediscovery. I have included only a small though varied sample of what is out there.

The authors range in period from the 1880s to the 1980s—from Frank Stockton to Diana Wynne Jones. Some are British, some are American; one is from Sweden. There are fairy stories and fantasies, tall tales, historical novels, ethnic novels, picture books, even a special kind of children's theater. Some of the books are obscure and long out of print. Others have a place in the standard histories of children's literature like the Meigs *Critical History*, *The Oxford Companion to Children's Literature*, and John Rowe Townsend's *Written for Children*. Some are even popular. All possess the historical importance, the high standard of craftsmanship, the richness of meaning, and the striking individuality to make them worthy of critical attention. Even the oldest and most obscure can, in my judgment, still be enjoyed by children, if some knowledgeable adult takes the trouble to perform an introduction.

Why have these particular works, as well as so many others, been neglected? Although it is much easier to say why a book basks in the limelight than why an equally fine book does not, some theories can be advanced.

Comedy, it has often been remarked, is a less respected mode than tragedy. Serious books and poems tend to get more respect—and much more analysis—than funny ones. While this is less true for children's literature, the generalization still has weight. The Newbery Award winners have certainly tended to be serious. More than one critic has pointed out how long it took Beverly Cleary to be considered for a Newbery—and how, when she did win the award, it was for the atypically serious *Dear Mr. Henshaw*. When humor is combined with a colloquial, unpretentious style, as it is in Cleary's work, the book is even less likely to be regarded as "important." These attributes fit several of the books and authors in *Rediscoveries*: not only Cleary's *Socks*, but Dorothy Canfield's *Made-to-Order Stories*, the fantasies of Diana Wynne Jones, and the Betsy-Tacy stories of Maud Hart Lovelace.

Fungus the Bogeyman by Raymond Briggs, *Island Mackenzie* by Ursula Moray Williams, and Frank Stockton's fairy tales are also funny, though in their case humor is compounded with an attribute that one might call "eccentricity." While all Briggs's picture books are unusual, *Fungus* is unquestionably the oddest. *Island Mackenzie* must be the only cat story ever written in the style of Victorian melodrama, which gives it an unsettling, though delightful, mock-heroic quality. Stockton's fairy tales wryly contradict one's expectations of what should happen in a fairy tale. Canfield's *Made-to-Order Stories* (unlike her *Understood Betsy*) are nearly impossible to "place" in terms of genre. Selma Lagerlöf's *Nils*, a bizarre combination of talking animal fantasy and social studies textbook, labors under the additional burdens of elaborate construction, awkward translation, and Swedish nationality.

Controversy may occasionally elevate a children's book to greater prominence, but more often becomes a handicap. The ethnic novels of Florence Crannell Means were highly regarded in the 1930s and 40s, but would have been too controversial for a Newbery Award at that time. Although one of her novels was designated a Newbery "Runner-up," only the actual Award winners have generally been publicized, listed, and kept in print. *Fungus the Bogeyman*, which is calculated to shock and repel adult readers, has also been tucked out of sight; as of this writing, it is Briggs's only picture book for children that is out of print in the United States.

Finally, none of these books has ever achieved universal popularity. *Fungus* never reached the huge audience that loved Briggs's *The Snowman*. *Socks* has always been less popular than Cleary's Ramona books. Even the fantasies of Diana Wynne Jones are popular only with children who have the reading ability and the intelligence to meet her challenges. There remains an ambivalence in the criticism of children's literature that hesitates to separate quality from popular appeal. Can a book be first-rate children's literature if it fails to capture large numbers of young readers?

Yet if the criticism of children's literature is ever to come of age, it must acknowledge the ultimate authority of the individual reader. If the *Morte Darthur* and the poems of Catullus can be considered first-rate literature on the strength of the small audience that continues to read and appreciate them, then the absolute number of children who still read Frank Stockton or Selma Lagerlöf should not matter either. It is the quality of their experience that counts. It does not even really matter whether the readers are adults or children. A good book is one that never loses its potential for rediscovery.

WORKS CITED

Carpenter, Humphrey and Mari Prichard. *The Oxford Companion to Children's Literature.* Oxford: Oxford University Press, 1984.

Mahony, Bertha E., and Elinor Whitney. *Realms of Gold in Children's Books.* Garden City, New York: Doubleday, Doran, 1929.

Meigs, Cornelia et al. *A Critical History of Children's Literature: A Survey of Children's Books in English.* Rev. ed. New York: Macmillan, 1969.

Nodelman, Perry, ed. *Touchstones: Reflections on the Best in Children's Literature.* 3 vols. West Lafayette, Indiana: Children's Literature Association, 1985–9.

Rahn, Suzanne. *Children's Literature: An Annotated Bibliography of the History and Criticism.* New York: Garland, 1981.

Townsend, John Rowe. *Written for Children: An Outline of English-Language Children's Literature.* 4th rev. ed. New York: HarperCollins, 1990.

Rediscoveries in Children's Literature

Life at the Squirrel Inn: Frank Stockton's Fairy Tales

> "I think," said the Sphinx, "that you have made your line
> long enough."
> "And I think," said the King, "that you made it a great
> deal longer than it need to have been by taking me about
> in such winding ways."
> "It may be so," said the Sphinx, with its mystic smile.
>   Frank Stockton, *"The Banished King"*

He is not only the first but one of the greatest American masters
of the fairy tale for children. Yet today he is known, if at all, by a
single short story for adults— "The Lady or the Tiger?"—and
two children's stories, "The Bee-Man of Orn" and "The Griffin
and the Minor Canon," which were resurrected only when
Maurice Sendak turned them into picture books. Sendak himself
confessed that for him Stockton "had always been, quite
honestly, 'The Lady or the Tiger?' man. I had never read
anything else. Reading 'The Griffin and the Minor Canon' was
very much like opening a treasure chest" (Stockton, *Griffin* 5).

Frank Stockton's treasure chest of fairy tales deserves re-
opening.[1] His blend of traditional folktale motifs and characters
with his own common-sense logic, quirky humor, and individual
philosophy is mellow and distinctive. Today's children should
enjoy the fun and invention of "The Griffin," "The Bee-Man,"
"The Floating Prince," "The Philopena," "The Magician's
Daughter," and "Prince Hassak's March" no less than children of
a hundred years ago. Older readers will appreciate their keen-
witted satire, and a sardonic view of life and human nature that
is still far from usual in children's literature.

Born in 1834, the son and younger brother of well-known crusading Methodists, Frank Stockton was not encouraged to become a fiction writer. After graduating from high school, he trained as a wood engraver, a "practical" trade at which he was no more than competent, and which was, ironically, soon to become technologically obsolete. In his spare time, however, he wrote stories and began to publish them, and by the 1870s was making a living as a free-lance writer and journalist. In 1873 he was hired as assistant editor to Mary Mapes Dodge, the founding editor of a new children's magazine, *St. Nicholas*.

Stockton helped to pilot *St. Nicholas* through its formative first five years, before ill health forced him to take a less strenuous position with *Scribner's Monthly*. Most of his writing for children continued to appear in *St. Nicholas* well into the early 1890s.[2] Besides fairy tales, he churned out nonfiction articles on science, travel, and history, translations of French and German stories and poems, a book of true pirate stories, and a historical novel with a medieval setting called *The Story of Viteau*. Much of this was hack-work—Stockton even had two pseudonyms to prevent his name from appearing too often in *St. Nicholas*—but nice, readable hack-work in a clear and easy-going style, with that characteristic air of good-humored rationality that Stockton maintains through his wildest imaginings.

He began publishing at a time when little fantasy had been written in America for children.[3] We have come to assume the pre-eminence of fantasy in children's literature, but in the era of William Dean Howells and Henry James, the typical children's story was set either in the here and now, or the here and when-I-was-your-age (like *Tom Sawyer*). In the *St. Nicholas* volumes of the 1870s and 80s, only a small percentage of the stories are fantasy or retellings of myths, legends, or folktales. Stockton became the first American author to make fairy tales for children his specialty, blazing a trail for the generation of Howard Pyle and L. Frank Baum.

Like Hans Christian Andersen and John Ruskin before him, Stockton seems to have taken off into fantasy straight from the folktales of Europe and the Near East that he had known as a child:

> I was very young when I determined to write some fairy tales because my mind was full of them. I set to work, and in course of time, produced several which were printed. These were constructed according to my own ideas. I caused the fanciful creatures who inhabited the world of fairy-land to act, as far as possible for them to do so, as if they were inhabitants of the real world. I did not dispense with monsters and enchanters, or talking beasts and birds, but I obliged these creatures to infuse into their extraordinary actions a certain leaven of common sense. (quoted in Griffin 11)

These first stories, featuring a diminutive fairy named Ting-a-ling, were published in 1870 as *Ting-a-ling* (and later renamed *Ting-a-ling Tales*). Compared to his later work, they are crudely done, with a boyishly violent humor. But the combination of "fanciful creatures" and "a certain leaven of common sense" was to permeate all of Stockton's fairy tales. Two volumes of these appeared in the following decade, *The Floating Prince and Other Fairy Tales* (1881) and *The Bee-Man of Orn and Other Fanciful Tales* (1887).

L. Frank Baum has been called the originator of a distinctly American fantasy for children, but the road to Oz runs through Frank Stockton country. Stockton employs a more traditional setting and cast of characters than Baum—small kingdoms with a medieval flavor and a chiefly prince-and-peasant population, plus a wide range of "fanciful creatures" from Greek and Near Eastern mythology and European folklore; fairies, dryads, sphinxes, afrits, wizards, dwarfs, giants, hobgoblins, genii, gnomes, griffins, and hippogriffs all mingle nonchalantly in the same landscape. His protagonists, whether princes or peasant girls (he is quite even-handed in his choice of sexes), are natives, able to encounter sphinx or fairy with a minimum of surprise. Baum enlists a far higher proportion of invented creatures, and plays off their oddity against astonished newcomers from our world. But his basic narrative strategy (as we see it in *The Wizard of Oz, The Road to Oz, The Lost Princess of Oz*, etc.) is very like Stockton's, and may have been learned from him: the naive protagonist journeying through strange lands and meeting a succession of eccentric yet generally sensible and friendly creatures, who often join themselves to the traveling party. And like Stockton, Baum makes a point of how such an assorted group can co-exist harmoniously. For both authors, fairyland is recognizably American, being both multi-ethnic (in its variety of creatures) and (despite the kings and queens) democratic; there is little of the bickering over status and power that goes on constantly in Lewis Carroll's worlds. While the "fanciful creatures" may play the traditional animal-helper role in assisting the protagonist on a quest, they also have independent "rights" as characters, with quests and motivations of their own.

Both Stockton and Baum, again, take great pleasure in imaginary inventions and labor-saving devices, such as were in real life the pride of pre-World War I America. Baum's prototype robot, the clockwork Tik-tok, would feel at home in the mechanical city of Stockton's "How the Aristocrats Sailed Away," which also must be wound up periodically to stay awake. Some of Stockton's stories, such as "A Tale of Negative Gravity" (1884) and "My Translataphone" (1900) (for adults) and "The Tricycle of the Future" (1885) (for children) are not even fantasy, but early technological science fiction. William Dean Howells, who found Stockton's work enjoyable but perplexing, complained that this "Edison" of authors presented human nature itself as "a cleverly put together toy"—that "the emotional element" was entirely absent from his stories, "except as it is supplied now and then by the inventor to lubricate his machinery a little" (136).[4]

For a novelist of character and emotion like Howells, this would be a fatal limitation, and Stockton's "straight" novels, though they have their defenders,[5] are not his most memorable work. For a writer of nonsense fantasy, however, it is logic, humor, and invention that are essential—character and emotion that must be subordinated to the smooth operation of the whole. Here Stockton, like Baum and Carroll, is superb.

Most Stockton fairy tales are based on familiar folktale patterns. The simplest stories are about children who encounter a "fanciful creature" near their own homes, and earn some reward from it through their own good will or good sense, like the folktale heroines of "Toads and Diamonds" or "Snow White and Rose Red." Selma is hired by gnomes as a tutor for their prince and takes home a generous salary in gold in "The

Emergency Mistress." Colin and his little sister win a Christmas decoration and a doll from the dwarfs in "The Sprig of Holly." The characters learn lessons that children can apply to their own everyday behavior. When a dwarf offers to exchange the only sprig of holly in the forest for a year of service, Colin sensibly refuses—and continues to refuse when the stakes are lowered to a month, a week, a day, an hour, or even a minute of absolute obedience.

> "A minute, then," said the dwarf.
>
> Colin hesitated. That was not a long time, but he might be made to fire a gun or do something very dangerous in a minute.
>
> "No, sir," said he.
>
> "A second?" cried the dwarf.
>
> "I might strike Dora in a second," thought Colin, and he sung out:
>
> "No, I won't." (*Floating Prince* 125)

Afterwards, his father praises him for his "'steady refusal to make a rash bargain, even for a very short time'" (128).

A larger, more complex, and more interesting group of stories includes "The Floating Prince," "The Magician's Daughter," "The Queen's Museum," "The Banished King," "The Philopena," and "Prince Hassak's March." Here the protagonists are of royal blood, their affairs involve whole kingdoms, and their quests take them far from home, where they may encounter not one but a whole menagerie of "fanciful creatures." These stories sometimes end in traditional fashion, with a royal wedding, and remind us of such folktales of quests and journeyings as "The Golden Bird," "The Water of Life," "The Fool of the World and the Flying Ship," or "The Seven Ravens."

The third group of Stockton's stories is the farthest from folktale origins and hardest to classify. These stories too may involve a journey and encounters with strange beings, but their protagonists are of lowly social status, with problems that are universal rather than royal—old age in "Old Pipes and the Dryad," fate in "The Bee-Man of Orn," the failure of goodness in "The Griffin and the Minor Canon." Their outcomes are not "happy endings." The Bee-Man ends exactly where he began, while "Old Pipes" and "The Griffin" conclude not with a wedding, but with the deaths of the dryad and the griffin who have befriended the protagonists.[6]

Like Andersen, Ruskin, Thackeray (in *The Rose and the Ring*), and Baum, Stockton built on traditional foundations of setting, characters, and plot. But in all his fairy tales, these traditional elements are outweighed by his consciously modern and critical approach to them. "I obliged these creatures to infuse into their extraordinary actions a certain leaven of common sense." The incongruity of common sense in a giant or a hippogriff becomes both a source of humor and a way of parodying the irrationality of the folktale. But the parody is affectionate. Unlike Mark Twain, Stockton felt none of that urge to destroy the European past that took form in *The Prince and the Pauper* and *A Connecticut Yankee at King Arthur's Court*. His *Personally Conducted*, a European travelogue published in *St. Nicholas* in 1887-8, encourages young readers to overcome their national prejudices and learn "new merits and virtues" from "the people we meet" in England, Germany, Italy, Switzerland, and France:

> The more the right kind of an American journeys the more he is likely to be satisfied that he is an American, but the better he becomes acquainted with other nations and learns not only to avoid their faults but to imitate their virtues, the greater advantage is he to his own country. (347)

Stockton's satirical targets only begin with the folktale; that same fondness for common sense leads him to poke fun at political systems, unrealistic social reformers, and human vanity itself. In "The Floating Prince," for example, Prince Nassime has been cast out of his kingdom by a usurper and decides to found a new realm of his own. "'The first person I meet,'" he declares, "'shall be my chief councilor of state, the second shall be head of the army, the third shall be admiral of the navy, the next shall be chief treasurer, and then I will collect subjects of various classes'" (*Floating Prince* 2). The first person he meets is a five-inch-tall fairy named Lorilla—who makes an excellent chief councilor. A giant becomes his general, a shepherd on stilts his admiral, a clam-digger his treasurer. A class of schoolboys is recruited to be

THE KINGDOM OF NASSIMIA AFLOAT.

An original illustration by E. B. Bensell for "The Floating Prince," first published in *St. Nicholas Magazine* 8, 2 (December 1880): p. 100.

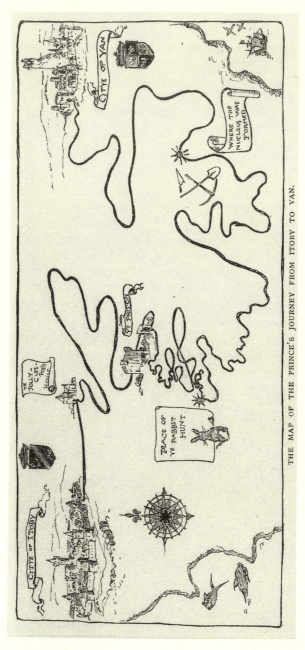

THE MAP OF THE PRINCE'S JOURNEY FROM ITOBY TO YAN.

A route that failed to "go straight." "Prince Hassak's March" may have been inspired by the Höllental Road in Germany, which was cut right through the rocks of the Black Forest to provide a straight route for Marie Antoinette on her journey from Austria to her marriage with the French dauphin. Reginald Birch's illustration was originally published in *St. Nicholas Magazine* 11, 2 (December 1883): p. 150.

the Prince's aristocracy, while a caravan of rich merchants and philosophers becomes his common people. The result of his random selections is a happy and prosperous community—with the implication that random selection might create a better society than our time-hallowed present system.

"The Clocks of Rondaine," published in 1887, satirizes the current passion for reform. Little Arla owns a beautiful clock which she is sure keeps perfect time. Disturbed by hearing the other clocks of Rondaine habitually striking the hour at disparate intervals, she sets off to persuade their owners to set them uniformly. She is disappointed to find no one willing to reset their clocks—and disconcerted when a kindly museum curator proves to her that her own clock is ten minutes slow.

Arla's is the innocent self-righteousness of a child, and Stockton is not hard on her. Arrogant adults, especially those with power, are fair game. The eponymous hero of "Prince Hassak's March" decides that it is "beneath the dignity of a prince" to be forced from his chosen path by natural obstacles. He declares that when he travels from Itoby to visit his uncle, the King of Yan,

> "Mountains and hills shall be tunneled, rivers shall be bridged; houses shall be leveled; a road shall be cut through forests; and, when I have finished my march, the course over which I have passed shall be a mathematically straight line." (141)

Accompanying Prince Hassak on his journey are a small army of laborers, three courtiers, two officers charged with setting his mathematically straight course by the stars and recording it on a map, and ten boys and girls from the schools of Itoby. For the prince wishes to show the children "how, when a thing was to be done, the best way was to go straight ahead and do it, turning aside for nothing" (141).

On the first day, all goes well, "with no further trouble than that occasioned by the tearing down of fences and walls, and the destruction of a few cottages and barns" (141). On the second day, the party comes to a rocky hill, on the top of which lives a jovial Jolly-cum-pop. He suggests that while the laborers drive a tunnel through the hill, the Prince and his party can join him on a hunt in the forest—but instead of finding game, the party itself is trapped by a jailer who needs prisoners to fill his empty cells. They escape with the help of some pigwidgeon fairies, wander lost and starving through the wilderness (failing to catch a rabbit), volunteer in exchange for food to "form the nucleus" of a new city, and finally make their way to Yan, marching into the city in their prison uniforms of bright green and yellow with large red spots. "'My dear Hassak,'" says the Prince's uncle, "'The next time you pay me a visit, I beg that, for your sake and my own, you will come in the ordinary way'" (150).

Back in Itoby at last, the map-maker shows the Prince the map he has made of the journey from Itoby to Yan—the course which was to be "a mathematically straight line."

> The Prince glanced at it and then he cast his eyes upon the floor. "Leave me," he said. "I would be alone." (150)

The story—whose twists and turns I have simplified—is typical Stockton in its inventiveness, its picaresque structure and varied characters, and its final irony. It is also typical in its criticism of foolish pride and the rigid pursuit of one's goal. Its hero is not the would-be heroic Hassak, but the Jolly-cum-pop, who accepts with unfailing good humor whatever life brings to him. Even finding himself the only prisoner too fat to escape through the narrow window of the jail does not trouble him:

> "It is the most ridiculous thing in the world," he said. "I suppose I must stay here and cry until I get thin." And the idea so tickled him, that he laughed himself to sleep. (144)

Later, when he has finally tired of the jail, he decides on a simple stratagem and easily frees himself. Back at home, he dismisses the prince's miners—who have succeeded in tunneling halfway through his hill—and converts the tunnel into convenient cellar space.

The journey through life expressed symbolically in "Prince Hassak's March" takes architectural form in *The Squirrel Inn* (1891), a novel for adults. The inn is a building of eccentric design, which exerts a peculiar and unsettling influence on the lives of its assorted inhabitants. Susan, the innkeeper's wife, is as frustrated as Prince Hassak when things don't turn out as she expects them to, and complains that "'nothing can go straight in a crooked house'" (198). To her husband, however, this is something to be grateful for:

> "It strikes me, Susan, that our lives are very seldom built with a hall through the middle and the rooms alike on both sides. I don't think we'd like it if they were. They would be stupid and humdrum. The right sort of a life should have its ups and downs, its ins and outs, its different levels, its outside stairs and its inside stairs, its balconies, windows, and roofs of different periods and different styles. This is education. These things are the advantages that our lives get from the lives of others.
>
> "Now, for myself, I like the place I live in to resemble my life and that of the people about me. And I am sure that nothing could be better suited to all that than the Squirrel Inn." (198).

To have succeeded in marching straight to Yan would have taught Prince Hassak nothing. His education springs from the unforeseen adventures that befall him—in fact, from the very failure of his quest.

Many of Frank Stockton's fairy tales tell of a quest that fails to "go straight," or even ends in failure. The Bee-Man's quest for a more impressive "original form" results in his becoming a humble bee-man again. The king in "The Banished King" sets out on his travels to learn how to rule more wisely, but becomes a perpetual wanderer, leaving his kingdom in the competent hands of his queen. Loris and Ninkum never do reach "The Castle of Bim," where everything is "'positively charming, and every body is just as happy and gay as can be'" (*Floating Prince* 186). As another character concludes, "'I don't believe any of us will find that place'" (198). In "The Sisters Three and the Kilmaree," Stockton even invents a boat that will not sail straight—the nautical equivalent of the Squirrel Inn:

> A kilmaree is a boat used exclusively by fairies, and is shaped a good deal like a ram's horn, with little windows and doors in various parts of it. The waters between the main-land and the island of the sisters were full of strange, entangled currents, and could be navigated only by a boat like a kilmaree, which could twist about as much as any current or stream of water could possibly twist or turn. Of

course these boats are very hard to manage, for the
passengers sometimes have to get into one door, and
sometimes into another; and the water sometimes comes
in at a front window and goes out at a back one, while at
other times it comes in at a back window and goes out at a
front one; sometimes the boat twists around and around
like a screw, while at other times it goes over and over like
a wheel, so that it is easy to see that any one not
accustomed to managing such boats would have a hard
time if he undertook to make a trip in one. (943)

Stockton's less fantastic tales often echo the same theme of
the quest that ends in failure. Arla fails to reform the clocks of
Rondaine. The boy inventor of "The Tricycle of the Future" sees
his invention destroyed. Several stories—including his fine
comic novel for adults, *The Casting Away of Mrs. Lecks and Mrs.
Aleshine*—deal with shipwrecks, a classic symbol for the random
destruction of human hopes and plans.

The theme is especially striking, however, in his fairy tales,
for in both traditional and literary fairy tales a quest that does
not succeed is a virtual self-contradiction. Nassime, in "The
Floating Prince," is an exception who proves the point; he gains
a kingdom for himself because he does not attempt to march
straight toward his goal, but "floats," learning from "the people
he meets" and the opportunities that come his way. "This," as
Frank Stockton says, "is education."

There is something stoical, in a pleasant way, about this
philosophy, and indeed, like many humorists, Stockton used
humor as a defense against his own melancholy. According to
his wife Marian, "He hated mourning and gloom. They seemed
to paralyze him mentally until his bright spirit had again
asserted itself and he recovered his balance" (Marian Stockton
206). And he spoke with intuitive understanding of the darkness
in his great contemporary Mark Twain:

It is well known that the actor of comedy often casts
longing glances toward the tragic mask, and when he has
an opportunity to put it on, he often wears it so well that
one cannot say that he has no right to it. The same pen-
point that will make a man laugh out in church, if gently
pricked by it, will not only slay a bride at the altar, but will

"THE BOAT BEGAN TO LOOK SOMETHING LIKE A KILMAREE."

A boat that cannot sail straight. An original illustration by E. B. Bensell for "The Sisters Three and the Kilmaree" from *St. Nicholas Magazine* 9, 12 (October 1882): p. 946.

"The Griffin sat looking at his image all the morning and all the afternoon." An original illustration by E. B. Bensell for "The Griffin and the
Minor Canon" from *St. Nicholas Magazine* 12, 12 (October 1885): p. 897.

go entirely through her and kill her father who is giving
her away. (quoted in Golemba 66)

In Stockton too, we occasionally feel the increased pressure
of the pen-point. Reading "The Lady or the Tiger?" we must
identify with a princess forced to choose between her lover's
marriage to another woman and his death. Stockton subtly
weights the story toward the tiger—then, by ending with the
famous question, forces us to articulate the choice ourselves.
And the underlying melancholy in some of his best children's
stories gives way to an even bleaker view of human nature in
"The Griffin and the Minor Canon."

Stockton wrote the story in Chester, England, inspired by
the strange wood and stone carvings of its ancient cathedral
(Marian Stockton 194). One day a Griffin comes flying out of the
wilderness, to a town whose church has a great stone griffin
carved above its porch; it is the Griffin's first chance to discover
what he looks like, for he has always lived alone. The
townspeople are terrified of the monster, and only one man
dares to approach and show him the statue. This is the Minor
Canon of the church— "a young man of a kind disposition"
(Stockton, *Griffin* 15) who is used to performing the duties no
one else cares for, conducting services for a weekday
congregation of three old women, visiting the sick and poor, and
teaching a school of bad children. But even after several days the
monster shows no sign of leaving. He has conceived a liking for
the Minor Canon, and begins to accompany him about his
duties.

As the autumn equinox approaches, when the Griffin is
known to take his semi-annual meal, the townspeople become
increasingly apprehensive. They order the Minor Canon to exile
himself to the wilderness, assuming that the Griffin will go in
search of him. Instead, the Griffin begins to take on some of the
Minor Canon's duties himself.

"It does not matter so much about the church," he said,
"for nobody went there; but it is a pity about the school. I
think I will teach it myself until he returns." (35)

The Griffin so terrifies the children that they work harder than
they ever have before.

> The Griffin used no severity toward them, but there was a
> look about him which made them unwilling to go to bed
> until they were sure they knew their lessons for the next
> day (38).

When the Griffin visits the sick, the effects are literally
"miraculous. All, except those who were very ill indeed, jumped
from their beds when they heard he was coming, and declared
themselves quite well" (38).

> As for the poor, they seemed to have utterly disappeared.
> All those who had depended upon charity for their daily
> bread were now at work in some way or other, many of
> them offering to do odd jobs for their neighbors just for
> the sake of their meals—a thing which before had been
> seldom heard of in the town. The Griffin could find no one
> who needed his assistance. (40)

When at last the desperate townspeople approach the
monster directly, he informs them that he despises them all far
too much to devour them:

> "They appear to be all cowards, and, therefore, mean and
> selfish. . . . In fact, there was only one creature in the
> whole place for whom I could have had any appetite, and
> that was the Minor Canon, who has gone away. He was
> brave and good and honest, and I think I should have
> relished him."
> "Ah!" said one of the old men very politely, "in that case I
> wish we had not sent him to the dreadful wilds!" (42–3)

Learning for the first time of the Minor Canon's
banishment, the Griffin is furious. He declares that he will find
the Canon and bring him back.

> "And if, when your Minor Canon comes back to you, you
> do not bow yourselves before him, put him in the highest
> place among you, and serve and honor him all his life,
> beware of my terrible vengeance! There were only two
> good things in this town: the Minor Canon and the stone
> image of myself over your church door. One of these you
> have sent away, and the other I shall carry away myself."
> (48)

Wrenching off the statue, the Griffin carries it to his cave. He finds the Minor Canon, dying of starvation, and nurses him back to health, then returns him to the town. Here the young man at last receives the treatment he deserves, and "before he died, he became a bishop."

The story ends,

> But they need never have been afraid of the Griffin. The autumnal equinox came round, and the monster ate nothing. If he could not have the Minor Canon, he did not care for anything. So, lying down, with his eyes fixed upon the great stone griffin, he gradually declined and died. It was a good thing for some of the people of the town that they did not know this.
>
> If you should ever visit the old town, you would still see the little griffins on the sides of the church; but the great stone griffin that was over the door is gone. (55–6)

Stockton may have meant "The Griffin and the Minor Canon" as a parody of such hero-versus-monsters legends as St. George and the Dragon. In his version, the monster is of nobler character than his potential victims; the hero triumphs not by an act of slaughter but by kindness, humility, and self-sacrifice; and the monster rescues *him*. Such a reversal would have been characteristic of Stockton's personal distaste for violent solutions. Stockton not only opposed the Spanish-American War (Golemba 31–2), but published a heartfelt pamphlet in 1860, urging that the South be allowed to secede peaceably from the Union (Golemba 28–9). His fiction includes such strongly pacifist works as (for adults) *The Great War Syndicate* (1889) and (for children) "Derido; or, The Giant's Quilt."

But the story's satire reaches deeper than parody. The townspeople seem to represent not merely such foolish individuals as Prince Hassak, but the generality of humanity—a cowardly, selfish, short-sighted humanity, willing enough to sacrifice their one hero, yet never appreciating what he is. Stockton underlines the indictment with sly jabs of his pen. These folk are afraid that the Griffin will devour their children, but ready "to mention that there was an orphan asylum in the next town" (42). Poverty, sickness, and naughtiness are impervious to the Canon's kindness, yet vanish with the first whiff of fear. Even the Griffin notices how irrelevant the church is to these people's lives (35). And though Stockton allows that in time they learned "to honor and reverence their former Minor Canon without the fear of being punished if they did not do so" (54), he ends by commenting, on the Griffin's death, that "It was a good thing for some of the people of the town that they did not know this."

The Minor Canon himself is Christ-like in his personal qualities, his self-imposed duties to the sick, the poor, and the outcast, and his rejection by the very folk he saves. His banishment recalls the traditional identification of Christ with the scapegoat, which is laden with the sins of the people and driven out into the wilderness (Leviticus 16: 8–10, 21, 22). Stockton's echoing of Biblical phrases— "their daily bread," "bow yourselves before him," "put him in the highest place among you" —and, of course, the presence of the church as setting for the story also guide the reader toward a religious interpretation. Stockton seems to suggest that Christian virtues are not truly valued, that if Christ reappeared he would once more be crucified by a stupid mob, and—since the Minor Canon ranks so low in the church hierarchy—that the religious establishment has lost sight of its own priorities.

But what, then, of the Griffin? If the Minor Canon represents Christ, one might expect him to vanquish a Devil-monster. This does not happen; instead, the Griffin saves his life and ensures his advancement. It is the Griffin, not the Minor Canon, who becomes the protagonist of the story and gives it its special quality. Again, as in "The Lady or the Tiger?" Stockton forces us to confront a monster—but the simple, savage tiger has been replaced by a creature whose complex form, half lion and half eagle, reflects its rich ambiguity.

The story begins and ends with the Griffin's statue. "In some way or other," says Stockton (explaining nothing), "the old-time sculptor had seen him, and afterward, to the best of his memory, had copied his figure in stone" (9). The statue is "not a pleasant one to look at," but impressive in its monstrous power, its "large head, with enormous open mouth and savage teeth," its "great wings" and long, barbed tail (7–8). Its placement above the very doorway of the church raises the question William Blake asked of the "Tyger":

> What immortal hand or eye
> Could frame thy fearful symmetry?

Surrounded by a myriad other sculptures of "saints, martyrs, grotesque heads of men, beasts, and birds" (8)—by all creation— the griffin suggests the untamed force of Nature, subject only to God the Creator. Indeed, as the Griffin's companion, the Minor Canon finds that the whole world of nature lies open to him:

> "It is like reading an old book," said the young clergyman to himself; "but how many books I would have had to read before I would have found out what the Griffin has told me about the earth, the air, the water, about minerals, and metals, and growing things, and all the wonders of the world." (30)

Yet the Griffin is neither all-knowing nor all-powerful. At the beginning of the story, he does not even know what he looks like. When he first arrives at the town, "His great wings were tired, for he had not made such a long flight in a century or more" (12). He has difficulty controlling his emotions; when he gets excited or angry, the barbed tip of his tail glows red hot, and he has to cool it in a stream (19). During his final, furious speech to the townspeople in the town hall, "the end of his tail was still so warm that it slightly scorched the boards as he dragged it after him" (47). Stockton has so vividly imagined his monster that he knows how awkward it would be for the Griffin to teach school from the Canon's desk, "his wide wings spread on each side of him, because he could not lean back in his chair while they stuck out behind" (36). Such details make the Griffin convincing, but also vulnerable. This terrifying monster cannot fit himself into human society any more than he can squeeze into the Canon's chair—and he is "the very last of his race" (9).

Ambiguity characterizes the Griffin's moral position too. He seems noble in his attraction to and appreciation for the Minor Canon, in his scorn for the townspeople, and his lofty refusal to take vengeance on them. Maurice Sendak clearly admires him. "Our friend the Griffin," he wrote, "is strong, proud, imperious, vain, intelligent, good—and, best of all, lionhearted" (Stockton *Griffin* 5). But the Griffin is not simply "good" like the Minor Canon. He *is* vain, especially in his fixation with the statue of himself, and we cannot overlook his intentions toward the Minor Canon:

> "Do you know," said the monster. . . , "that I have had, and still have, a great liking for you?"
>
> "I am very glad to hear it," said the Minor Canon, with his usual politeness.
>
> "I am not at all sure that you would be," said the Griffin, "if you thoroughly understood the state of the case. . . ."
> (51)

Surely the Griffin's assumption that he has the right to devour the Minor Canon is the height of egotism—yet it does not strike us, somehow, as wholly outrageous or impossible. In the above passage, and elsewhere, Stockton plays with the close relationship between the language of food and the language of love. ("'In fact, there was only one creature in the whole place for whom I could have had any appetite. . . . I think I should have relished him,'" says the Griffin. And again, "'Now, I had conceived a great liking for that young man, and had intended, in a day or two, to go and look him up.'") Ingestion is, after all, an act of union, and there is a strange interdependence between the young man and the monster. For all his goodness, the Minor Canon is ineffective without the Griffin's help; it is the Griffin who succeeds in curing the sick, teaching the bad children, and banishing poverty from the town. But it is the Minor Canon who inspires the Griffin to carry on his work, and without him, in the end, the Griffin can find no reason to live. "If he could not have the Minor Canon, he did not care for anything" (55). Each needs the other to make himself complete—as the spiritual and the animal make up the fully human being. Was Stockton suggesting, long before the Jungians, that we need the primitive strength and natural, instinctive wisdom of the animal within ourselves?

Or was he aware of the traditional symbolism associated with the griffin, that made its likeness appropriate for a cathedral? In Christian iconography, the griffin, half eagle and half lion, symbolized the union of two natures in Christ—the divine (bird) and the human (animal). (So a griffin appears in Canto 29 of Dante's *Purgatorio*, drawing the triumphal chariot of Beatrice.) But it was not necessary for Stockton to have learned this in order to see his own Griffin as something monstrous, yet divine. Between them, the Griffin and the Minor Canon may represent two aspects of a God Stockton had known all his life—the terrifying Jehovah of the Old Testament and the self-sacrificing Jesus of the New. It fits perfectly that the townspeople do not honor the Minor Canon for his own sake, but only when the Griffin's "terrible vengeance" threatens them. They need a God of Fear—and it is just as well that they do not realize when that God is dead.

Though "The Griffin and the Minor Canon" has always been a favorite with children, it is Stockton's darkest fairy tale. It portrays human nature as cowardly, selfish, and despicable, incapable of appreciating either the simple goodness of the Minor Canon or the rich mysteries of meaning summed up in the Griffin. And it suggests that something of value is diminishing, withdrawing forever into the wilderness. It ends not with the Minor Canon's elevation to a bishopric—which we could accept as a happy ending—but with the Griffin's lonely death and the disappearance of the great statue from the church. Its last word is "gone."

Stockton himself, who took pleasure in writing fairy tales and counted the best of them among his finest work, wondered if they could really be for children (Marian Stockton 193), and clearly they are not for children alone. But children deserve the chance to enter Stockton's world—to enjoy his humor, puzzle over his logic, share his sardonic view of human society. They need at least one author to tell them, in a dry and pleasant fashion, of the pitfalls that lie in wait for idealists and reformers, of the frustration and failure they will all encounter in the years ahead—and of the compensations of life at the Squirrel Inn.

NOTES

1. There are encouraging signs of revived interest in Stockton's fairy tales. Two paperback collections have recently been published: *Fairy Tales of Frank Stockton*, edited by Jack Zipes (1990) and *The Lady or the Tiger and Other Stories*, edited by Jane Yolen (1992). Several collections of Stockton's short stories for adults are also in print, along with the two picture books illustrated by Maurice Sendak, *The Griffin and the Minor Canon* and *The Bee-Man of Orn*.

2. The bibliography of Stockton's short stories for children is complex and confusing, for although he published only four collections of stories in addition to *Ting-a-Ling* and *Ting-a-Ling Tales*, many stories appear in more than one of these collections. Martin Griffin lists all the stories in each collection in his *Frank Stockton*; so does Jack Zipes in *Fairy Tales of Frank Stockton*. In order of their publication, the other four collections are

The Floating Prince and Other Fairy Tales (1881).

The Bee-Man of Orn and Other Fanciful Tales (1887).

The Queen's Museum (1887).

The Clocks of Rondaine and Other Stories (1892).

It is clearly false that Frank Stockton stopped writing for children after the success of his adult novel *Rudder Grange* in 1879, contrary to *The Oxford Companion to Children's Literature* (see its article on Stockton, page 497).

3. Nathaniel Hawthorne's *Wonder-Book* (1851) and *Tanglewood Tales* (1853), which do pre-date Stockton's work, are retellings of traditional material rather than original fairy tales. For an authoritative survey of early American fantasy for children, see Mark I. West's *Before Oz: Juvenile Fantasy Stories from Nineteenth-Century America*.

4. In "Fiction, New and Old," *Atlantic Monthly* 87 (January 1901): 136–7. Other articles by Howells on Stockton include "Stockton and His Works," "Stockton's Stories," and "A Story-Teller's Pack."

5. Notably among today's critics, Henry L. Golemba, whose *Frank Stockton* (1981) is the most interesting recent study of Stockton's work. I am indebted to his book for calling my attention to *The Squirrel Inn*.

6. The only unambiguously happy ending in this unorthodox group of tales belongs to "The Poor Count's Christmas," published in *St. Nicholas* 9 (Dec. 1881–Jan. 1882). Impoverished by his own charities, Count Cormo sells his bed rather than forego his annual Christmas party for the local children; with the help of a quickwitted fairy and a

goodhearted young giant, the children surprise the Count with an enormous Christmas tree laden with furniture and bags of gold. The giant becomes his adopted son, and "'What a happy Christmas I have had!' said good Count Cormo" (193). Despite this positive *dénouement*, the realistic description of genteel poverty at the beginning of the story sounds a melancholy note that (for me, at least) pervades the whole.

WORKS CITED

Golemba, Henry L. *Frank Stockton*. Boston: Twayne, 1981.

Griffin, Martin I.J. *Frank Stockton: A Critical Biography*. Philadelphia: University of Pennsylvania Press, 1939.

Howells, William Dean. "Fiction New and Old." *Atlantic Monthly* 87 (January 1901): 136–7.

———. "Stockton and His Works." *Book Buyer* 20 (February 1900): 19.

———. "Stockton's Stories." *Atlantic Monthly* 59 (January 1887): 130–32.

———. "A Story-Teller's Pack." *Harper's Weekly* 41 (May 29, 1897): 538.

Stockton, Frank. "The Banished King." *St. Nicholas* 10, 1 (December 1882): 118–26.

———. *Fairy Tales of Frank Stockton*. Ed. Jack Zipes. New York: Penguin, 1990.

———. *The Floating Prince and Other Fairy Tales*. New York: Scribner's, 1881.

———. *The Griffin and the Minor Canon*. Introduction by Maurice Sendak. New York: Holt, Rinehart and Winston, 1963.

———. *The Lady or the Tiger and Other Stories*. Ed. Jane Yolen. New York: Tor, 1992.

———. "The People We Meet." *Personally Conducted. St. Nicholas* 15, 1 (March 1888): 347–53.

———. "The Poor Count's Christmas." *St. Nicholas* 9 (December 1881–January 1882): 122–7; 189–93.

———. "Prince Hassak's March." *St. Nicholas* 11, 1 (December 1883): 141–50.

———. "The Sisters Three and the Kilmaree." *St. Nicholas* 9, 10 (October 1882): 943–52.

————. *The Squirrel Inn. The Novels and Stories of Frank Stockton.* Vol. 2. New York: Scribners, 1899–1904.

Stockton, Marian. "A Memorial Sketch of Mr. Stockton." *The Novels and Stories of Frank Stockton.* Vol. 23. New York: Scribners, 1899–1904.

West, Mark I. *Before Oz: Juvenile Fantasy Stories from Nineteenth-Century America.* New York: Archon, 1989.

Wild Models of the World: The Lure of the Toy Theater

> ... the toy theater,—there it is, with its familiar
> proscenium, and ladies in feathers, in the boxes!—and all
> its attendant occupation with paste and glue, and gum,
> and water colours, in the getting up of the Miller and his
> Men, and Elizabeth, or the Exile of Siberia. . . . a teeming
> world of fancies so suggestive and all-embracing. . . .
>
> Charles Dickens, *"A Christmas Tree"*

> We never know how much of our after imaginations
> began with such a peep-show into paradise.
>
> G.K. Chesterton

A lively John Leech engraving, from a series entitled "Young Troublesome, or Master Jacky's Holidays," shows a group of delighted children, two girls and two boys, to whom a tall gentleman with elegant side-whiskers presents what looks to us like a good-sized television set. The caption, however, informs us that "Here Captain Clarence arrives with the Theatre Royal Drury Lane in miniature, and the Miller and his Men in a forward state of preparation." It is 1845, and the tall gentleman's gift—a fitting emblem of the difference between childhood then and now—is not a television but a toy theater.

For those who study children's literature, the toy theater offers territory all but untouched, yet full of possibilities. It is a form of imaginative play, an elaborate toy, a species of drama, a phenomenon of popular culture, a rich source of material on the Romantic theater, an unexpected influence on Victorian literature. Historically, it was one of the earliest genres of children's literature to aim squarely at entertainment. Considered as a branch of children's theater—the "Juvenile Drama" was its other name—it was unique in adapting a wide range of plays originally designed for adults to performance by and for children. Its young devotees included not only future men and women of the theater (Henry Irving, John Gielgud, Ellen Terry, Ralph Richardson), but artists (Millais, Frith, Beardsley, Dicky Doyle), writers (Dickens, Stevenson, Lewis Carroll, Masefield, Valéry, the Sitwells, G.K. Chesterton)—even Winston Churchill. "He was a jolly and impulsive lad," reminisced the toy theater tradesman/publisher H.J. Webb, "and I shall never forget the way he would vault over my counter" (quoted in Speaight 182).

What was the special appeal of the toy theater to these and thousands of other children? What made Master Jacky's performance of that toy theater classic *The Miller and His Men* the high point of his holidays?[1]

A toy theater is a miniature theater, tabletop size, in which plays are produced for the amusement of one's friends and family. The actors are tiny, brightly painted figures two or three inches high, cut out of paper and mounted on thin cardboard. Several figures in different poses are used to represent each of the main characters in a play. Some young producers (including Doyle and Beardsley) drew their own characters and even made up their own plays, but the common practice was to buy printed sheets of the characters, props, and scenery for each production, along with specially adapted scripts. The expression "penny plain and twopence colored" originated with the toy theater, for each play was available in both hand-colored and uncolored versions.

Set in tin "slides"—stands to which long wires are attached—the actors are pushed from the wings into the stage area, where they can move about freely and even duel with each other. In his definitive *History of the English Toy Theatre*, George Speaight explains that "The toy theatre convention is to indicate which character is speaking by a slight movement of its slide, the degree of movement depending upon the emphasis of the speech; this may seem silly at first, but one very soon accepts it as perfectly natural" (108).

Here Captain Clarence arrives with the Theatre Royal Drury Lane in miniature, and the Miller and his Men in a forward state of preparation.

From *Young Troublesome, or Master Jacky's Holidays* by John Leech, 1845.

A typical sheet of characters designed to be colored and cut out for a toy theater performance. Notice that the same character may be depicted in several different poses, so that he can "perform" various actions in the play. *Pizarro, or The Spaniards in Peru* was adapted from the Richard Sheridan play first performed in 1799. From *The History of the English Toy Theatre* by George Speaight (Boston: Plays, Inc., 1969).

For decades, all toy theater plays were based on real-life theatrical productions. Such juvenile favorites as *The Miller and His Men*, *Guy Fawkes*, *Pizarro*, *Black-eyed Susan*, *Jack Sheppard*, *The Forest of Bondy*, and *Timour the Tartar* were originally full-sized hits, whose colorful costumes, lavish scenery, and spectacular stage effects were faithfully reproduced in miniature. Even the toy theater "Cinderella" was adapted from the Rossini opera *La Cenerentola* (1817), and "Aladdin" from a "Grand Romantic Spectacle" performed at Covent Garden in 1826.[2] Those interested in the popular Romantic stage will find, Speaight says, that "A little imagination, or better still a histrionic manipulator, will complete the charm and re-create before us, tiny but perfect, the theatre of the years between 1810 and about 1850" (33).

Speaight traces the origins of the toy theater to the full-length portrait prints of actors in their current roles that first became popular around 1800. Next came prints showing all the principal characters in a production (first seen in 1811), then prints showing both characters and scenery which might be cut out and set up to reproduce the high points of a play—perhaps even used to present crude performances (1812). The final step was the manufacture of toy theater stages and publication of "Juvenile Drama" scripts specially condensed and otherwise adapted for toy theater production—an evolution complete by 1835.

Only gradually, Speaight stresses, did the toy theater become a toy. The early theatrical prints were intended for adult fans, and even the miniature theaters were at first a hobby for young men and older boys. (They continued to be considered a boy's toy, though a few girls had their own theaters, and in some families brothers and sisters worked together on the productions.) In Regency England, moreover, even a boy of ten might be a seasoned theater-goer. Contemporary evidence suggests that "visits to the theater were unusual, but not unknown, for a child of six, and usual for children of twelve" (Speaight 91). Jane Austen attended *Midas* and the pantomime *Don Juan* with her twelve and thirteen-year-old nieces (Speaight 91). In *Vanity Fair* (set, at this point, in 1826), eleven-year-old Georgy Osborne and his friend "visited all the principal theatres of the metropolis" and "knew the names of all the actors from

Drury Lane to Sadler's Wells" (Thackeray 618). Naturally, the boys also performed "many of the plays to the Todd family and their youthful friends, with West's famous characters, on their pasteboard theatre" (618).

The plays of 1810-1850 were simple, relying on moral melodrama, visual spectacle, and hearty humor. Though not designed for children, they were not difficult for children to understand or enjoy, and they adapted easily to the particular strengths and limitations of the toy theater. As G.K. Chesterton explains,

> In a small theatre, because it is a small theatre, you cannot deal with small things. . . . You can introduce a dragon; but you cannot really introduce an earwig; it is too small for a small theatre. And this is true not only of small creatures, but of small actions, small gestures and small details of any kind. (quoted in Ward, 260–1).

That perennial favorite *The Miller and His Men*, originally a play by Isaac Pocock performed in 1813, features a wealthy miller (Grindoff) who is in reality the leader of a band of robbers, his abduction of the innocent Claudine, a gallant young man (Lothair) who infiltrates the band to save Claudine, and the attack of Count Fribourg and his soldiers on the mill. "'Surrender,' cries the Count. 'Surrender?' answers Grindoff with a terrible snarl. 'Surrender? Never! I have sworn never to descend from this spot alive!'" (Speaight 182).[3] "Loud explosions" are heard, and the miller's rejected mistress (Ravina) blows up the mill with Grindoff and his men trapped inside. Grandiose speeches, great sweeping gestures, dramatic tableaux, scenic spectacles, mind-boggling special effects—all were equally characteristic of the Romantic stage and of the toy theater.

Clearly, the toy theater's intimate relationship with the full-sized stage could not survive the growing dominance later in the century of tea-table comedy and the social problem play— of Wilde, Shaw, and Pinero. Tied to its traditional repertoire, the Juvenile Drama began to seem not only juvenile but old-fashioned. Competition from the more elaborate German theaters, cutthroat price wars between English publishers, and an increasingly wider choice of hobbies for children are other reasons suggested by Speaight for the decline of the English toy theater. A few publishers continued to reprint the old plays into the twentieth century, but no new plays were brought out in the traditional style.

Yet children and, increasingly, nostalgic adults still played with toy theaters. Collectors were beginning to seek out the best of the old sheets. Appreciative essays were written by G.K. Chesterton and Robert Louis Stevenson. "The Juvenile Drama had no sooner died," says Speaight, "than people began to wonder if it could be revived" (175). Both Jack Yeats (brother of the poet) and J.B. Priestley tried their hand at original toy theater scripts, and Speaight describes a brave attempt by the Bumpus bookstore in the 1930s to market the traditional plays and stages—an attempt in which he himself played a part, with his well-reviewed public performances of *The Corsican Brothers*, *The Miller and His Men*, and *The Sleeping Beauty*. And in the 1960s, the shop of the last surviving publisher, Benjamin Pollock, found a new purchaser and set up business once again, selling the old-style stages, reprinting some of the old plays, and displaying a fine collection of antique stages and other toys as Pollock's Toy Museum. On this mildly hopeful note, Speaight's history ends.

For those of us with no opportunity to become acquainted with the toy theater in childhood, Speaight is invaluable. His is the bone-deep, lifelong knowledge for which no amount of research can substitute; he was ten when he put on his first toy theater plays. Built on this foundation of experience and buttressed by research, his *History* is solid, meticulous, and convincing. His enthusiasm, keen visual sense, and zest for detail—and the unobtrusive grace and humor of his style—give it charm. The various toy theater publishers—West, Webb, Pollock, Hodgson, Skelt, and Green—are presented with affection as individual, often eccentric personalities, characters in a drama of their own.

Yet in his concern to trace the main descent of the toy theater from prints intended for adults, Speaight gives only desultory attention to the part played in its parentage by children's literature. Only four pages of the chapter "Georgian Home Amusements" are devoted to children's paper toys that he considers in some way "forerunners" of the toy theater—"turn up" flap picture books based on Harlequin's adventures, paper doll cut-out books, and movable pictures. Without contesting his basic theory of origins, we might want to examine more closely the relationship of the toy theater to the general development of children's literature during the Regency.

Peter Haining's *Movable Books: An Illustrated History* makes clear that a wide variety of such books was already available in the early nineteenth century. Several of his examples bear some resemblance to the miniature stage settings of the toy theater: "slot books," in which tiny cut-out figures were slotted into pictorial backgrounds; "peep-shows," which folded out into three-dimensional scenes; and "panoramas," some of which featured cut-out figures to be fitted into three-dimensional backgrounds. Considered in this context, the toy theater seems less isolated as a phenomenon. The range of related toys suggests a period of freewheeling experimentation in ways of combining elements of story with the visual and tangible.

We can also connect these experiments with paper toys to the minor flowering in children's literature described by Iona and Peter Opie in *A Nursery Companion*, a compilation of Regency children's picture books. It was during the brief period of the Regency that children's literature, soon to wither in a cold blast of Victorian utilitarianism, first ventured into nonsense poetry, brightly colored illustration, even (with such poems as "A Visit from Saint Nicholas") fantasy.[4] The newly invented toy theater must have been a part of this burst of playful energy. And with its unabashed use of color, fantasy, exotic settings, and wild adventures, it may well have helped "set the stage" for the later nineteenth-century flowering of children's literature that we call the Golden Age.

Not only the toy theater's descent from the full-sized adult stage but its close kinship with the world of children's books is important if we want to analyze its significance for the children who played with it. On this point Speaight has little to conjecture. For him, the toy theater is essentially the early nineteenth-century Romantic stage in miniature form; he can only suggest that its Romanticism may still infuse "our sober northern blood" with "bright 'twopence coloured' images in the fog, exaggerated shadows like caricatures, a touch of drama, a brave and boyish romance, the breath of poetry" (182). He notes,

Scene 1st **SKELT'S SCENES IN HARLEQUIN & LITTLE TOM TUCKER.** *Nº1*

Jersey, Pub.ᵈ by G.SKELT, 2ᴬ, Clearview Sᵗ Saint Helier.

A sheet of scenery, showing the backdrop for Scene I of *Harlequin and Little Tom Tucker*, adapted from a pantomime of 1845. Here the romance of the frozen North mingles with the fantastic and grotesque. From the collection of the author.

in support, the "romantic strain" conspicuous in Robert Louis Stevenson and G.K. Chesterton, two lifelong lovers of the toy theater.

Stevenson and Chesterton themselves have contributed illuminating essays on what the toy theater meant to them as children. Stevenson's "A Penny Plain and Twopence Coloured" (1884) appears in *Memories and Portraits*, and has been included with the scripts of some of Pollock's toy theater plays in recent years, as a kind of testimonial. Remembering Skelt as the principal publisher during his own youth, Stevenson calls the special quality of the toy theater "Skeltery." "What am I?" he asks, "what are life, art, letters, the world, but what my Skelt has made them? He stamped himself upon my immaturity. The world was plain before I knew him, a poor penny world; but soon it was all coloured with romance" (225). The toy theater initiated Stevenson into Romanticism. He "met there the shadows of the characters I was to read about and love in a late future; got the romance of *Der Freischutz* long ere I was to hear of Weber or the mighty Formes; acquired a gallery of scenes and characters with which, in the silent theatre of the brain I might enact all novels and romances . . ." (226).

Stevenson's response to the toy theater was emotional and imaginative, Chesterton's more intellectual and spiritual. In the second chapter of his *Autobiography*, Chesterton traces his philosophical preference for "frames," "limits," and "bridges" to his childhood experience of toy theater plays produced by his father. In his essay "The Toy Theatre" (in *Tremendous Trifles*), he contends that "All the essential morals which modern men need to learn could be deduced from this toy" (121). One moral is that "Art is limitation" (121), as the small frame of the stage limits what we see:

> This strong, square shape, this shutting off of everything else is not only an assistance to beauty; it is the essential of beauty. The most beautiful part of every picture is the frame. (121–2)

Another "moral" is that "You can only represent very big ideas in very small spaces." Because the toy theater is small, "it could easily represent the Day of Judgment" (122). Both Stevenson and Chesterton, in their different ways, see the toy theater as a kind of window into a world paradoxically larger and more meaningful than the "penny world" of everyday life— a window opening through the imagination of a child.

Examining the reminiscences scattered through Speaight's *History* and A.E. Wilson's *Penny Plain, Two Pence Coloured: A History of the Juvenile Drama* (1932), we find another paradox: that these loving memories of the toy theater have no necessary connection with its supposed function—the performance of a play. Stevenson, for example, cheerfully confesses that although he enjoyed coloring the scenery and characters, he felt no urge to put on the play they belonged to:

> Yes, there was pleasure in the painting. But when all was painted, it is needless to deny it, all was spoiled. You might, indeed, set up a scene or two to look at; but to cut the figures out was simply sacrilege; nor could any child twice court the tedium, the worry, and the long-drawn disenchantment of an actual performance. Two days after the purchase the honey had been sucked. (219–220)

A.E. Wilson quotes this passage and comments, "Alas! I am afraid that is the true description in the experience of most. . . . in the many years of devotion to the cardboard drama I cannot recall that I ever actually completed the production of or went through a whole performance of any play" (21).

Clearly, a toy theater performance presents great technical difficulties for the young producer. Dickens, though an enthusiast as a boy, refers sadly in "A Christmas Tree" to the "besetting accidents and failures" of the toy theater, "particularly an unreasonable disposition in the respectable Kelmar, and some others, to become faint in the legs, and double up, at exciting points of the drama" (10–11). The rapid entrances and exits of characters in their various poses, combined—usually by a single performer—with dialogue, lighting, music, special effects, and changes of scenery, are challenging even for an adult to coordinate. To Speaight, J.B. Priestley admitted that "he and Sir Cedric Hardwicke had been completely unable to make head or tail of the toy theatre that I myself had proudly sold him" (106).

Even Chesterton, who as an adult constructed his own toy theater in which to perform plays for children, swears that he "worked much harder at the toy theatre than I ever worked at any tale or article" (120). "If I am ever in any other and better world," he wrote, "I hope that I shall have enough time to play with nothing but toy theatres; and I hope that I shall have enough divine and superhuman energy to act at least one play in them without a hitch" (121). Taking issue with Wilson's assessment, Speaight insists that he knows "several boys, even in the twentieth century, who have staged successful performances" (106). For him, the printed sheets of characters "only really fulfil their destiny and come alive upon the stage itself" (107). Yet he too concedes that "a smooth and finished toy theatre performance requires a great deal of rehearsal and is really an altogether adult venture" (106). The superb photograph (Figure 16 in the *History*) of the adult Speaight in the throes of such a performance speaks for itself.

For the young producer, the performance, even if finally achieved, was often Stevenson's "long-drawn disenchantment." John Oxenford, a nineteenth-century drama critic of the London *Times*, attests that

> The actual performance was not a very brilliant affair, the only persons really amused being the manager and his assistants, if he had any, so that yawns were frequent among the audience long before the final descent of the curtain. The dialogue read in a schoolboy voice became lamentably dull as the piece proceeded, and to fancy that it was uttered by those flat Lilliputians who glided over the stage was beyond the power of the most unbridled imagination. (quoted in Speaight, 105-6)

In short, to make the toy theater do what it was presumably designed to do was for many children—even older children—extremely difficult, and if achieved, disappointing. We must seek elsewhere for the appeal that made it a favorite recreation for generations. Again, it is the candid Stevenson whose essay suggests a solution to the mystery. He writes that in the stationer's shop where he bought his new plays as a boy,

> Every sheet we fingered was another lightning glance into obscure, delicious story; it was like wallowing in the raw stuff of story-books. I know nothing to compare with it save now and then in dreams, when I am privileged to

read in certain unwrit stories of adventure, from which I
awake to find the world all vanity. . . . (216–7)

The purchase and the first half-hour at home, that was the
summit. Thenceforth the interest declined by little and
little. . . . (218)

Parents used to complain; they thought I wearied of my
play. It was not so: no more than a person can be said to
have wearied of his dinner when he leaves the bones and
dishes; I had got the marrow of it and said grace. (220)

Finally, he says, he derived intense enjoyment from merely
poring over the names of plays on the publisher's list. He
remembers "one sequence of three from that enchanted calendar
that I still at times recall, like a loved verse of poetry: *Lodoiska,
Silver Palace, Echo of Westminster Bridge*. Names, bare names, are
surely more to children than we poor, grown-up, obliterated
fools remember" (221).

For young Stevenson the toy theater was primarily an
imaginative stimulus, "the raw stuff of story-books," whose
pictured characters and scenery and "bare names" did not so
much *satisfy* his imagination as set it vigorously to work. And
this, I suspect, was true for many other, less gifted children as
well. Oxenford too writes that "In my day the preparation for the
performance gave infinitely more pleasure than the performance
itself, and the gift of a theatre with a piece that could be acted at
once, would have been regarded with the indifference with
which an angler would contemplate a basket of killed fish
offered as a substitute for his expected day's sport" (quoted in
Speaight, 102). And dramatist-critic William Archer does not
hesitate to claim that "It is precisely because performances never
came off that the toy theatre is so infinitely preferable to its
so-called real rival. . . . It is the very gymnasium of the
imagination" (quoted in Wilson, 24).

The "sport" of the toy theater was both occupation for the
hands as the child colored, cut out, and mounted the paper
figures and scenery, and an invitation to the imagination to
create stories with them. Some children, like Stevenson, might
find sufficient stimulus in studying titles and printed sheets and
perhaps coloring the scenes and characters. Others might need to
cut out and arrange the figures, or even to attempt production of

the play. Still other children might create their own plays. At all levels of participation the magic of the toy theater was equally effective.

Indirect evidence to support this theory can be found in the poor literary quality of toy theater scripts. The original plays on which toy theater plays were based were for the most part moral-formulaic melodramas or simple-minded pantomimes. Even when the original was itself of high quality—for example, Shakespeare or, at a further remove, the plays based on Scott's novels or *Der Freischutz* or *Oliver Twist*—not much was likely to survive the minifying process. According to Speaight, a toy theater performance should last no longer than half an hour (108), and "normally the cutting was ruthless" (96).

The final text might consist largely of stage directions, as in this passage from Green's *Jack Sheppard*:

> Scene 33. Four Cells in Newgate. Jack discovered chained.
>
> *Jack.* I will try to get myself free again. I can but die! (Jack to be drawn off behind the chimney, and Jack, Fig. 2, to come in his place.) I have broke part of my irons; one more effort. (To be drawn off as before, and Jack, Fig. 3, to take his place.) I have succeeded; now to get one of the bars from the chimney. (To be drawn off as before; the bricks from the chimney to fall, to be done by the trick in the Set Piece, plate 2. Jack, Fig. 4, to appear with iron bar.) (quoted in Speaight, 96)

Chesterton does not seem to have been greatly exaggerating when he asserts that in the toy theater,

> everything dramatic should depend not on a character's action, but simply on his appearance. Shakespeare said of actors that they have their exits and their entrances; but these actors ought really to have nothing else except exits and entrances. The trick is so to arrange the tale that the mere appearance of a person tells the important truth about him. (quoted in Ward 261)

The exigencies of toy theater production reduced all plays to a standard style and structure. Since formula dominated to this extent, we may usefully compare the appeal of toy theater plays to that of other kinds of formula fiction that succeed with

children: comic books; series books like "Nancy Drew" or Enid
Blyton's "Famous Five" or the "Choose Your Own Adventure"
books. It was, I believe, Wallace Hildick, in *Children and Fiction*,
who first postulated that children enjoy such fiction differently
from works of literary quality (see his Appendix D). Hildick
argues that the very dominance of the formula and absence of
stylistic interest encourage children to use formula fiction as a
basis for their own daydreams and imaginings. The experience
offered to young readers by formula fiction is different in kind
from that offered by good literature—but valuable in its own
way, as a kind of exercise routine for the imagination.

By this yardstick, one routine is as good as another. Any
formula that children enjoy will do. Yet since formula fiction not
only stimulates but directs the imagination, different formulas
may guide it in very different directions. And the particular
combination of qualities bound up in the traditional toy theater
is one that enlarges a child's experience in ways that Enid Blyton
and Nancy Drew do not.

The toy theater is first of all, as Speaight and Stevenson
attested, a kind of elementary education in the Romantic—in a
way of looking at nature and supernature, love, heroism, and
history. Speaight's appendix of play titles, listing the authors
from whose works the plays were adapted, is enough to make
his point. However dramatized, oversimplified, and condensed,
major works of Romanticism from *The Castle of Otranto* to *Uncle
Tom's Cabin* found their way onto the miniature stage; their
authors included Sir Walter Scott (pre-eminent, with eleven
different works adapted for the toy theater), Ossian, Prosper
Merimée, Dumas *pére*, Peacock, Byron, Fenimore Cooper,
"Monk" Lewis, La Motte-Fouqué, Southey, even Coleridge (with
Remorse). A kind of Romantic poetry, as Stevenson testified,
sounds even in the titles of plays long forgotten:

- The Hag of the Lake, or The Castle of Monte Falcon
- The Temple of Death
- The Blood Red Knight, or The Fatal Bridge
- Sixteen-String Jack
- The Vision of the Sun
- Korastikan, Prince of Assassins, or The Dreaded Harem

- The Skeleton Horseman
- The Prince, or The Illuminated Lake
- The Tiger Horde
- The Gnome King, or The Giant Mountains
- The Wild Boy of Bohemia
- Zoroaster, or The Spirit of the Star.

And while the literary quality of the scripts was not high, costumes and scenery were often visually exciting, works of Romantic stage art in their own right.

That the original plays were written primarily for adults also gives the toy theater a special value. Toy theater plays push gently and enticingly against the boundaries of what was (and is) considered appropriate for children. Married love and the conflict between law and justice (in *Black-eyed Susan*), a plot to overthrow the government (in *Guy Fawkes*), a villainous but fascinating king (*Richard III*) or criminal (*Jack Sheppard*, *Dick Turpin*, and many more), the downfall of an empire (*Pizarro*), the loss of a man's soul (*The Devil and Doctor Faustus*), revenge and erotic love (*Mazeppa*)—these are not found frequently in children's literature. As Chesterton pointed out, it is not small things but large ones that work best in the toy theater.

There is no modern equivalent for this amalgamation of children's literature, adult theater, and creative toy. Clearly, the toy theater is not a nineteenth-century TV. It engages actively both the hands and the creative imagination of the child; even the watching audience must use its imagination to make the tiny figures come alive. If we find it difficult to visualize our own children playing with such toys, perhaps we are simply underestimating what childhood can be.

It is, at least, still possible to find a traditional toy theater to try out on a contemporary child.[5] Pollock's flourishes as a combination shop and toy museum at The Market in Covent Garden, and is worth a visit if you are in London. You can see there on display the very toy theater—a small "Britannia" model—which hung from the ceiling of Mr. Pollock's shop a hundred years ago, and on which the man-grown Stevenson used to bump his head when he came through the door, revisiting his beloved "twopence coloured" world.

NOTES

1. Two other engravings in "Master Troublesome" show Jacky and his brothers and sisters cutting and pasting the "scenes and characters," and Jacky (with the help of two younger brothers) performing *The Miller and his Men* for an audience of children and servants. Most boys would *probably* not have fired off a real pistol to represent the explosion of the mill.

2. See the notes to *Cinderella; or, The Little Glass Slipper* and *Aladdin; or, The Wonderful Lamp*, reissued by Pollock's Toy Museum and Theatres in 1961 and 1963 respectively. The toy theater also borrowed extensively from Romantic painting and other visual arts for its sets and costumes. In "The Brigand in the Toy Theatre," George Speaight traces the history of a typical toy theater production—Pollack's version of *The Brigand*—back to its origins in an 1829 play by James Robinson Planché, a series of paintings by Charles Eastlake, and an 1828 engraving entitled "Distant View of Naples."

3. George Speaight suggests that Winston Churchill, whose favorite toy theater play was *The Miller and his Men*, may have borrowed unconsciously from Grindoff's defiant speech for his own great speech of 1940: "We shall fight on the beaches, we shall fight on the landing grounds, we shall fight in the fields and in the streets, we shall fight in the hills: we shall never surrender!" (*History* 182).

4. According to the Opies, "the sparkle of the Regency extended even to the trappings of the nursery. The children's books produced in the first quarter of the nineteenth century have an alertness and grace not achieved in any other period. . . . But the temper of the times was soon to change. . . . By 1832 and the no-nonsense days of the Reform Bill, the inhabitants of the nursery were once again being looked upon as little pudding-bags to be stuffed with knowledge" (7).

5. The closest contemporary equivalent to the traditional toy theater that I have seen is *Dracula: A Toy Theatre*. This oversize, spiral-bound book reproduces Edward Gorey's Tony Award-winning sets, props, and characters from the 1977 Broadway production. Although there is no stage, no script (only a synopsis), and no way of moving the characters about, children are encouraged to "stage your very own miniature production of this classic vampire tale." *Petrouchka: A Ballet Cut-Out Book* is also based on a real full-size production. Its sets and costumed figures by Jane F. Kendall echo the original 1911 designs of Alexandre Benois, and there is a detailed synopsis by Leonard S.

Marcus. Neither of these can really be called a *theater*; they would be more accurately classified as "panoramas."

WORKS CITED

Aladdin; or, The Wonderful Lamp. London: Pollack's Toy Museum and Theatres, 1963.

Chesterton, G.K. *Autobiography*. New York: Sheed and Ward, 1936.

———. "The Toy Theatre." *Tremendous Trifles*. New York: Sheed and Ward, 1909.

Cinderella; or, The Little Glass Slipper. London: Pollack's Toy Museum and Theatres, 1961.

Dickens, Charles. "A Christmas Tree." *Christmas Stories*. The New Oxford Illustrated Dickens. Vol. 13. Oxford and London: Oxford University Press, 1948-58.

Gorey, Edward. *Dracula: A Toy Theatre*. New York: Scribner's, 1979.

Haining, Peter. *Movable Books: An Illustrated History*. London: New English Library, 1979.

Hildick, Wallace. *Children and Fiction*. London: Evans, 1970.

Kendall, Jane F., and Leonard S. Marcus. *Petrouchka: A Ballet Cut-Out Book*. Boston: Godine, 1983.

Opie, Iona, and Peter Opie. *A Nursery Companion*. London: Oxford University Press, 1980.

Speaight, George. "The Brigand in the Toy Theatre." *The Saturday Book* 29 (1969): 205–15.

———. *The History of the English Toy Theatre*. Boston: Plays, Inc., 1969.

Stevenson, Robert Louis. "'A Penny Plain and Twopence Coloured.'" *Memories and Portraits*. New York: Scribners, 1897.

Thackeray, William Makepeace. *Vanity Fair: A Novel without a Hero*. New York: Heritage Press, 1940.

Ward, Maisie. *Gilbert Keith Chesterton*. New York: Sheed and Ward, 1943.

Wilson, A.E. *Penny Plain, Two Pence Coloured: A History of the Juvenile Drama*. New York: Macmillan, 1932.

The Boy and the Wild Geese: Selma Lagerlöf's *Nils*

> When the miners heard the words, they thought it was
> their own longing that made the goose-cackle sound like
> human speech. "Take us along with you!" they cried. "Not
> this year," shrieked the boy. "Not this year." (I, 373)[1]

The boy is fourteen-year-old Nils Holgersson. Diminished to thumb-size by an angry elf, he has joined a flock of wild geese led by the famous Akka from Kebnekaise on their spring migration to Lapland, riding the back of his parents' big white gander. At the beginning of his journey, Nils is "an all-round good-for-nothing . . . cruel to animals, and ill-willed toward human beings" (I, 6). When he returns home in the fall, he has escaped the jaws of bears and foxes, saved an old castle from an invasion of rats, seen the Great Crane Dance, rescued a little boy from drowning, closed a dead woman's eyes, been kidnapped by crows, made friends with eagles, storks, and ravens, and traveled the full length of Sweden. His adventures have developed his courage and initiative, sharpened his wits, and given him the capacity to love and care for others—both human beings and animals.

When Selma Lagerlöf published the first volume of *Nils Holgerssons underbara resa genom Sverige* in 1906, it quickly became Sweden's bestseller of the year. Reviews hailed it as equal to or surpassing the earlier works of Scandinavia's most famous woman novelist, soon to be winner of the Nobel Prize for Literature (1909).[2] Less than a year after its publication, *Nils* had been translated into Danish, German, and English. The second volume appeared in 1907; in English, the two volumes were published as *The Wonderful Adventures of Nils* (1907) and *Further Adventures of Nils* (1911).

Nils remains a highly reputed classic in its native country, reinterpreted by new generations of illustrators, translated into film, even set to music as an opera.[3] The boy on the goose's back is everywhere—etched in fine crystal, pictured on packets of stationery, woven in straw to make a Christmas ornament. In England and America, historians of children's literature still praise *Nils* highly. Elizabeth Nesbitt discusses it at some length as one of the great fantasies of the early twentieth century in *A Critical History of Children's Literature*. *The Oxford Companion to Children's Literature* calls it a "strikingly original work" that "remains one of Sweden's outstanding contributions to children's literature" (578). Roger Sale offers an interesting analysis of its opening chapters in *Fairy Tales and After*.

Yet Nils is little known in America today, even among adults with a professional or scholarly interest in children's books. Its length, its complex narrative structure, and its challenging vocabulary place it outside the reading range of the nine to twelve-year-olds who were its original audience. The archaisms of Velma Swanston Howard's 1907 translation with its "thees" and "thous" and "right merrilys" are another obstacle.[4] So is the unfamiliarity of the Swedish setting, with its strange names and geography. Its age and its nationality—neither British nor American—tend to exclude it from standard lists and surveys.

And the world of children's literature is rich in animal fantasy. What makes *Nils* worth the extra trouble to seek out and introduce to children? What makes it irreplaceable?

Nils's story begins not with some lucky child listener like Alice Liddell or Alastair Grahame or Josephine Kipling, or with a writer reliving childhood, but with the National Teachers Association of Sweden. It was their idea to commission from their most famous novelist a supplementary reader for use in the public schools. The book, as they envisioned it, would give Swedish children a deeper knowledge and appreciation of their own land—its folklore, its wildlife, its geography, and the

"The wild geese were lined up, with Akka in the lead, and were marching toward him with great solemnity"

An illustration by Astri Heiberg from the original edition of *Further Adventures of Nils* (New York: Grosset and Dunlap, 1911).

principal landmarks, products, and historical sites of each region. Of course, it was to be a work of art as well.

Selma Lagerlöf had never written anything for children, and the task that had been given her seemed impossible. For nearly a year, she thought about the book without being able to write a line of it. "At last," she tells us in a surprisingly self-referential episode near the end of *Nils* itself,

> she became so tired of the whole thing that she said to herself: "You are not fitted for such work. Sit down and compose stories and legends, as usual, and let another write this book, which has got to be serious and instructive, and in which there must be not one untruthful word." (II, 294)

Lagerlöf also tells us in this episode how the dilemma was resolved. Seeking for inspiration to break through her writer's block, she revisits her beloved childhood home, the country estate Marbacka, which had been sold years ago. In the garden, she chances upon "a tiny midget, no taller than a hand's breadth, struggling with a brown owl" (303). She rescues him from the owl, and he tells her the whole story of his adventures. "'What luck to run across one who has travelled all over Sweden on the back of a goose!' thought she. "Just this which he is relating I shall write down in my book"' (II, 304)—the very book we are reading now.

It seems likely that an actual visit to Marbacka was transformed into this magical encounter. Such a visit would have triggered vivid childhood memories—among them, perhaps, that story told her as a little girl, about a gander that flew off with the wild geese one spring and returned to Marbacka in the fall, bringing a wild mate and children with him. In real life, there was no Nils to save the trusting geese from being butchered, but as a novelist Lagerlöf could remake the past and give the story a happy ending.[5] That same year, with her earnings as a writer, she was able to buy back Marbacka for her own, and change the ending of her childhood too.

Inventing Nils enabled Lagerlöf to write in the way that was natural to her, as a storyteller, while incorporating the masses of factual material that her assignment required. The marvel is that the book soars so far above its utilitarian origins.

Information about Swedish wildlife becomes a series of life-and-death encounters with allies and enemies. Geographical information comes to life in local legends that Nils recalls or overhears; Smaland's lack of natural resources, for example, is explained by the tale that this province was created not by God but by the unpracticed and incompetent St. Peter (I, 301-8)! Some legends are related with great dramatic power; "The Animals' New Year's Eve" and "The Dream" achieve a near mythic resonance. The descriptions of fields, forests, marshes, cities, and seacoasts that Nils visits or flies over have the richness and intensity of poetry, and no two are alike. Avoiding the threadbare and unconvincing device of an omniscient companion—one of the wild geese, perhaps—able to answer Nils's every question, Lagerlöf allows her protagonist to make his own observations, combining what he sees and overhears with the scrappy bits of knowledge that a lazy schoolboy might actually possess.

Like some of its own landscapes, the highly episodic *Nils* resembles an immense patchwork quilt rather than a conventionally coherent novel. Yet it possesses not only the individual beauties of its many parts, but a kind of unity in the very diversity it celebrates—the unity in diversity that is Sweden itself.

Nor could Lagerlöf limit herself to the assignment outlined by the Teachers Association. Like all great fantasies, *Nils* reifies the intensely personal vision of its author. Lagerlöf's own preoccupations with humanity's relationship to the natural world, the tension between tradition and progress, and the process of spiritual redemption become "wonderful adventures" too.

Although Lagerlöf's animals can talk to each other, her natural world has the feel of reality. No less an authority than Konrad Lorenz, the founder of animal ethology, writes in *King Solomon's Ring* of the "most beneficial" influence of her work and Kipling's on his mental development as a child. Both authors, he says,

> convey a true impression of what a wild animal is like, although they are telling fairy tales. . . . one feels that if an experienced old wild goose or a wise black panther could

talk, they would say exactly the things which Selma
Lagerlöf's Akka or Rudyard Kipling's Bagheera say. (xviii)

Again, in *The Year of the Greylag Goose*, Lorenz testifies to the
essential truth of *Nils*. "There happens," he says, "to be one
writer I know of whose artistic talent does justice to the romantic
aura of migratory birds and who portrays their precarious and
heroic existence with great skill: Selma Lagerlöf" (172).

Her animal world is harsher than those of Kenneth
Grahame, E.B. White, or even Beatrix Potter, for the relationships
between species and with human beings are not idealized. The
goose flock—including Nils himself—is in constant danger from
predators both animal and human; the domestic animals, though
safe from wild beasts, are at the mercy of their often selfish and
unthinking masters. Death hangs over all the characters, animal
and human. The crow Garm Whitefeather falls in the moment of
triumph; the elk Grayskin is hunted to his death by poachers;
Nils's former companions Osa and Mats lose their entire family
to tuberculosis, and then Mats, too, is killed; the old peasant
woman dies alone in her little cabin, mourned only by her cow.
Nils himself learns that he will be unable to return to human
form unless he brings back the white gander to be slaughtered.
The ever-present possibility of a tragic outcome heightens
suspense throughout the book, for one cannot feel sure that any
character, except Nils, will survive. Yet the novel, though deeply
emotional and sometimes very painful reading, is neither
depressing nor sentimental. Its characters meet their fate
uncomplaining, with heroic pride or, more often, quiet stoicism.
When Nils tells the old cow that her mistress is dead, she says
simply,

> "Then it will soon be over for me as well." "There will
> always be someone to look out for you," said the boy
> comfortingly. "Ah! you don't know," said the cow, "that I
> am already twice as old as a cow usually is before she is
> laid upon the slaughter-bench. But then I do not care to
> live any longer, since she, in there, can come no more to
> care for me." (I, 359)

In episodes like this, Lagerlöf suggests an essential kinship
between human beings and animals, and the kind of relationship
that should grow from it. Like humans, animals suffer, mourn,

and die; Lagerlöf surmises that animals may even possess a rudimentary sense of the numinous, a "longing after the unattainable, after the hidden mysteries back of this life," which stirs in them when they see the cranes dance in the spring (I, 156). For both animals and humans, implacable fate can be mitigated by love. Love can cross the barriers between species: Nils's growing love for his goose-comrades, Akka's fostering of the young eagle Gorgo, Grayskin's friendship with the dog Karr, the old cow's love for her mistress.

Yet too often human beings fail to recognize the kinship and misuse their fellow creatures. Like Nils, they must learn compassion. The family that cages a wild squirrel, unthinkingly separating her from her young, realizes in the end that "'we, on this farm, have behaved in such a manner that we are shamed before both animals and human beings'" (I, 79). A couple supporting the plan to drain Lake Takern, where thousands of waterfowl make their homes, think better of it when their own little son is lost there. Searching and crying for him, the boy's mother hears the cries of the wild birds, and "the anguish which she herself was suffering, opened her heart."

> She thought that she was not as far removed from all other living creatures as people usually think. She understood much better than ever before, how birds fared. They had their constant worries for home and children; they as she . . . .
>
> Then she happened to think that it was as good as settled that these thousands of swans and ducks and loons would lose their homes here by Takern. "It will be very hard for them," she thought. "Where shall they bring up their children now?" . . .
>
> She remembered how on the following day the proposition to lower the lake was to be decided, and she wondered if this was why her little son had been lost—just to-day.
>
> Was it God's meaning that sorrow should come and open her heart—just to-day—before it was too late to avert the cruel act? (405-6)

Selma Lagerlöf's position in 1906 was remarkably close to that of today's conservationists. She too argued that wild creatures have a right to live, and that sufficient habitat for their survival should be set aside for them. Akka's farewell to Nils, at the end of the book, makes her views explicit:

> "If you have learned anything at all from us, Thumbietot, you no longer think that the humans should have the whole earth to themselves," said the wild goose, solemnly. "Remember you have a large country and you can easily afford to leave a few bare rocks, a few shallow lakes and swamps, a few desolate cliffs and remote forests to us poor, dumb creatures, where we can be allowed to live in peace. All my days I have been hounded and hunted. It would be a comfort to know that there is a refuge somewhere for one like me." (II, 322)

Lagerlöf's vision of the kinship between animals and human beings is linked to the theme of progress, and the tension between past and future. For her animals also seem to represent the human race at an earlier, more primitive stage of development. The human characters, while often selfish or callous, are also peaceful and civilized. They are shown farming, going to school or church, working in mines and factories, studying their own history. The animals, on the other hand, are constantly fighting, feuding, stalking, and killing one another; only the religious truce of the Great Crane Dance once a year calls a temporary halt to their perpetual inter-species warfare.

Their desperate struggles and tragic fates are reminiscent of Scandinavia's Heroic Age. Smirre Fox carries on a relentless blood-feud with Akka and Nils. Garm Whitefeather, like Hamlet, must play the fool to hide his true fitness for crow-kingship from the pair who have usurped his rightful place in the flock; and like Hamlet, he is killed before he can assume his "throne." The last surviving black rats are besieged in a castle by their relentless gray kinsmen. As in the Norse sagas, outlawry is a punishment for the most heinous crimes. Smirre Fox is outlawed by his fellow foxes when he breaks the truce of the Great Crane Dance to attack the geese. When Grayskin the elk accidentally steps on a snake and kills it, the snake's mate vows revenge; in the end, Grayskin is forced into exile, where he is hunted and killed by poachers. Co-existing with a modern, peaceful Sweden, the animal realm retains the ethos of the heroic but ruthless past.

Lagerlöf's conservationist vision cannot be confused with a desire to preserve the past in Sweden. Romantic though she is, she does not believe in going backward. Nils refuses to destroy the ironworks that are driving the bears from their last stronghold, even when Father Bear threatens him with death. Nils also fails to rescue the beautiful old city of Vineta, which sank beneath the ocean centuries ago and rises for only one day every hundred years. Saddened by his inability to break the spell, he eventually comes to see that "it was better that it should remain in all its glory down in the deep" (I, 298). "But when people are old," Lagerlöf comments dryly, "and have become accustomed to being satisfied with little, they are more happy over the Visby that exists, than over a magnificent Vineta at the bottom of the sea" (I, 298).

Throughout *Nils*, Lagerlöf shows how each of Sweden's diverse provinces has achieved its own prosperity in modern times. But she also relates legends and traditions that define each province's special character. While recognizing the tension between progress and tradition, she attempts to find a balance— to preserve something of the past, of wild nature, legend, and folk tradition, while embracing "the Visby that exists" in the peace and prosperity of today.

The most obvious thematic thread in *Nils*—the process of spiritual redemption—is closely woven together with the others I have discussed. The good-for-nothing boy must learn to feel compassion for both animals and human beings. Yet his experience of the primitive world of nature also makes him appreciate for the first time what it means to be civilized and human. These interconnections were not new in children's fantasy; Charles Kingsley had worked out a similar pattern in *The Water-Babies* (1863). Lagerlöf herself had traced the process of sin and redemption in several of her novels for adults, including her famous *Gösta Berling's Saga* (1891). Nils's slow, gradual, and logical change of heart, however, is unusually convincing.

The first step occurs immediately after his transformation, when his own family's domestic animals treat him with open hostility and refuse to help. Angry, and momentarily forgetful of his new size, Nils tries to pull the cat's tail as he has done so often in the past. The cat promptly pounces on him, opening its jaws across his throat.

> The boy felt how the sharp claws sank through his vest and shirt and into his skin; and how the sharp eye-teeth tickled his throat. He shrieked for help, as loudly as he could, but no one came. He thought surely that his last hour had come. Then he felt that the cat drew in his claws and let go the hold on his throat.
>
> "There!" he said, "that will do now. I'll let you go this time, for my mistress's sake. I only wanted you to know which one of us two has the power now." (21)

Even Nils realizes how foolish it was to mistreat the animals now that he is at their mercy; self-interest alone, in the absence of any higher motive, suggests that treating others decently is good sense.

This sharp lesson is followed by the chance of a fresh start in a new community, the flock of wild geese. Again, simply in order to survive, Nils must change his behavior. At the end of the first day's journey, he realizes that the white gander is all he has, and drags the exhausted bird into the water. In return, the gander finds him a fish to eat and suggests that Nils come along to help him on the way to Lapland. Nils must also prove to the wild geese that he can be useful to them before they will accept him. So he saves one of the flock from Smirre Fox, carries her babies to the imprisoned squirrel, and rescues the gander from a farm family which has captured him. But what begins as self-interest grows into true loyalty and even love; by chapter 8 there is already a real bond between the boy and his new companions.

At this point, his eagerness to accompany the geese is still a sign of how far, emotionally, he still has to go. "It was a strange thing about that boy—as long as he had lived, he had never cared for anyone," explains Lagerlöf. "Therefore there was no one whom he missed or longed for" (I, 109). In chapter 3, when Akka persuades the elf to give Nils back his human form if he will return home at once, the boy is not delighted but disappointed. "'I don't want to be human,'" he cries. "'I want to go with you to Lappland'" (I, 109).

By chapter 6, however, he is missing the sound of human voices. He wanders through a cathedral town at night, admiring the intelligence and power and spiritual hunger that it reveals. He sees a pretty young girl leaning over a balcony, and "a strange anxiety" comes over him, "as though he wanted to weep" (I, 164). "Nils Holgersson had not understood what he was losing when he chose to remain an elf; but now he began to be dreadfully afraid that, perhaps, he should never again get back his right form" (I, 166).

His sorrow, in chapter 14, for the lost city of Vineta is unmotivated by any possible benefit to himself, and represents another step upward. The shame and grief he feels in chapter 16, on briefly encountering his old playmates Osa and Mats, show for the first time that human relationships have become important to him. And his vigil over the dead peasant women in the following chapter—an act of charity toward a stranger— brings the change to full consciousness. When he learns from the cow how her dead mistress had yearned for her lost children, all emigrants to America, he suddenly realizes that his own parents may be longing for him too.

> This thought made him happy, but he dared not believe in it. He had not been such an one that anybody could long for him.
>
> But what he had not been, perhaps he could become. (I, 367)

From this moment, Nils wants to go home again, and he becomes a helper of human beings as well as animals.

What Lagerlöf shows us in Nils is a kind of moral evolution—from loving animals, to loving human beings, and finally to the love of goodness for its own sake. In *Further Adventures*, Nils discovers that he cannot break his word even to escape from captivity (II, 170). He can even be merciful to his bitter enemy, Smirre Fox (II, 238). And when he learns that the elf's new condition for changing him back into human form is to "'bring back Morten Goosey-Gander that your mother might lay him on the block and chop his head off'" (II, 287), he resolves to go on wandering with the wild geese forever rather than betray his friend. Even when he is told that his parents are in financial straits and may have to sell their farm, he replies unswervingly, "'My father and mother are square and upright folk. I know they would rather forfeit my help than have me come back to them with a guilty conscience'" (II, 315). Fortunately, the conditions fulfill themselves. The gander returns on his own and is promptly seized for slaughter; Nils rushes into the cottage to save him, and finds himself his right size once more. He comes home fully redeemed, with integrity as well as love.

A final and satisfying complexity of this complex book is the ambivalence of its final scene. Nils meets the wild geese once more, but finds that he can no longer speak their language. He strokes and pats them in farewell, then walks away, aware of the gulf between their kind and his. "He knew perfectly well that the sorrows of the birds do not last long, and he wanted to part with them while they were still sad at losing him" (II, 339). His love, his understanding, and his acceptance at this moment are those of a fully mature adult. Yet his last thought, as he sees them fly away from him, is that "he almost wished he were Thumbietot again and could travel over land and sea with a flock of wild geese" (II, 339).

Selma Lagerlöf does not pretend that we can have it all—childhood and adulthood, irresponsibility and maturity, past and present, the animal world and the world of humankind. We must make our choices, and with each choice we lose as well as gain. It is only our own longing that makes the goose-cackle sound like human speech. Only in the realm of fantasy will the geese take us along with them this year.

Notes

1. All quotations from Nils are taken from the original American editions. Quotations from *The Wonderful Adventures of Nils* are followed by the Roman numeral I and the page number. Quotations from *Further Adventures of Nils* are followed by the Roman numeral II and the page number.

2. Not all critics reacted favorably. For a summary of outraged contemporary responses to *Nils*, see Nils Afzelius, "The Scandalous Selma Lagerlöf."

3. The opera, *Nils Holgersson*, was premiered by the Värmland Music Theatre in 1986, with a libretto by Eva Strandin and music by Bjorn Kruse. See Knud Ketting, "The Wonderful Adventures of Nils" in *Nordic Sounds*.

4. In 1991, a new paperback edition of *The Wonderful Adventures of Nils* was published by Skandisk in Minneapolis, based on the old Howard translation but "revised" by Nancy Johnson. Although this revision has its own awkward spots, it does away with Howard's conspicuous archaisms, and is much more accessible to modern readers. The back cover carries enthusiastic recommendations from, among others, the children's author Astrid Lindgren and the president of the University of Minnesota.

5. Lagerlöf retells the story as "The Gander" in *Marbacka*.

WORKS CITED

Afzelius, Nils. "The Scandalous Selma Lagerlöf." *Scandinavia* 5, 2 (November 1966): 91–9.

Ketting, Knud. "The Wonderful Adventures of Nils." *Nordic Sounds* (March 1987): 2–4.

Lagerlöf, Selma. *Further Adventures of Nils*. Translated by Velma Swanston Howard. New York: Grosset and Dunlap, 1911.

———. *Marbacka*. Translated by Velma Swanston Howard. Garden City, New York: Doubleday, Page, 1925.

———. *The Wonderful Adventures of Nils*. Translated by Velma Swanston Howard. New York: Grosset and Dunlap, 1907.

———. *The Wonderful Adventures of Nils*. Translated by Velma Swanston Howard. Rev. by Nancy Johnson. Minneapolis: Skandisk, 1991.

Lorenz, Konrad. *King Solomon's Ring*. Translated by Marjorie Kerr Wilson. New York: Thomas Y. Crowell, 1952.

———. *The Year of the Greylag Goose*. New York: Harcourt Brace, 1979.

Sale, Roger. *Fairy Tales and After: From Snow White to E.B. White*. Cambridge: Harvard University Press, 1978.

Empowering the Child: Dorothy Canfield's *Made-to-Order Stories*

> For an instant Betsy gazed into those clear eyes and then
> ... why, gracious goodness! That was herself she was
> looking at! How very, very different she looked from the
> last time she had seen herself in a big mirror! She
> remembered it well—out shopping with Aunt Frances in a
> department store, she had caught sight of a pale little girl,
> with a thin neck, and spindling legs half-hidden in the
> folds of Aunt Frances's skirts. But she didn't look even like
> the sister of this browned, muscular, upstanding child
> who held Molly's hand so firmly.
>
> Dorothy Canfield, *Understood Betsy*

In *Understood Betsy*, a sickly, fearful little girl is transformed into a sturdy, self-reliant one. It's not hard to trace where the idea came from. In 1912, two years after the birth of her first child, Sally, the American novelist Dorothy Canfield visited Maria Montessori's school in Rome, where she was particularly impressed by the mature and self-reliant behavior of the children.[1] In 1912 she published *A Montessori Mother*, an account of her visit and an introduction to Montessori principles. In 1913, the year of her second child Jimmy's birth, her *Montessori Manual* explained how these principles might be applied in American families. Next came a series of articles in *To-day's Magazine*, expanded in book form as *Mothers and Children* (1914). Designed for the general public, the articles stirred up a small storm of controversy by arguing that unquestioning obedience was not the chief (or even a desirable) goal of child-rearing (see Fisher 114–6). Canfield refused to retract her position, and went on to

51

publish *Self-Reliance: A Practical and Informal Discussion of Methods of Teaching Self-Reliance, Initiative and Responsibility to Modern Children* in 1916.

In the meantime, she was beginning to incorporate Montessori principles into her fiction as well. Sylvia's childhood in *The Bent Twig* (1915) is a Montessori ideal brought to life (Washington 70). Sylvia and her sister participate in adult activities and discussions, and mother, father, and children all do the housework together. Years later, as a young woman, Sylvia can resist the materialism and corruption of society, thanks to her lifelong habit of independent thought and judgment.

A logical next step was to address children directly. *Understood Betsy* was serialized in *St. Nicholas* in 1916 and published the following year. As Nancy Romalov has shown, a 1915 visit to Park School in Buffalo played an important part in its creation. The experimental school strongly resembled an old-fashioned country home, in which children were given real, meaningful work to do and made to feel part of the adult world. Here was a way for Canfield to connect the Montessorian "educational future" to her treasured Vermont heritage. To effect Betsy's transformation, there was no need to send her to a special Montessori school, simply to move her from an up-to-date home and school in the city, to an old-fashioned home and one-room country school in Vermont.

In 1916, with *Understood Betsy* completed, Canfield and her two children sailed to France, where her husband John had joined the Ambulance Service and was now at the front (Washington 87–88). Her war years, a time of anguish, intense activity, and personal change, effectively ended Canfield's "Montessori period." Her continuing espousal of Montessori principles is clear, however, in such later works as *The Home-Maker* (1924), a novel for adults, and *Fables for Parents* (1937), a collection of short stories. She remained one of the few novelists in any period to write deeply and thoughtfully of the experience of parenthood and of good and bad child-rearing.

Understood Betsy has recently enjoyed something of a revival, with new editions in hardcover and paperback.[2] Few of its admirers have even heard of Dorothy Canfield's very different yet equally innovative second book for children, *Made-to-Order Stories* (1925).

In a letter to her publisher, Alfred Harcourt, Canfield described how these stories first came to be told and written down, and what they were. For "years now," she wrote,

> ever since Jimmy could talk, we have "run" a series of what we call "Jimmy's made-to-order stories." He hates the banality of the usual book-story where he sees from afar the same old tricks about to be turned, and invented this way of getting stories that are bound to be unexpected. He gives his own recipe— "I want a story with a puppy and an ice-berg and a churn and a little boy and a dozen marbles." Thus avoiding the usual story of a puppy with a tin-can tied to its tail and a brave little boy-scout who rescues the poor thing which turns out to belong to the millionaire Lady Bountiful of the village or something of that sort. You can imagine that stories constructed with the ingredients which Jimmy gives out, are unexpected if nothing else. The whole point about them is that the unexpectedness must be in the incidents and not in the telling which is always matter-of-fact and serious. It has made a little narrative recipe which has amused Jimmy and Sally for a long time. I must have told a thousand of them, more or less. They run off as fast as you can talk, you know, since you are bound by none of the usual rules of narrative. Well, in Switzerland, last Christmas time, I happened to tell one about an angry polar bear which got the children to laughing so that they had the idea of setting it down for other children to laugh over. (Quoted in Washington 171)

Canfield was doubtful whether the story would work when "decanted into cold print," or for an audience outside the family circle. But she wrote down "The Angry Polar Bear," plus four others told during the next four days, and had them tried out by Mildred Batchelder on the children of the Horace Mann School; if the stories went well, she decided, they could be submitted to *St. Nicholas* (Washington 171).[3] Yet despite the enthusiasm of the Horace Mann children, the letter to Harcourt shows her still dubious about the stories: "Personally, I haven't the least idea whether they're not too trivial to consider. John thinks I've taken leave of my senses to have written them down at all" (Washington 172).

There is often good reason to wonder whether stories told spontaneously to one's own children will "decant" well for anyone else's. But Dorothy Canfield had additional cause to doubt. These "made-to-order stories" were radically different from anything she had published, including her one other book for children.[4] *Understood Betsy*, like Canfield's novels for adults, is serious realistic fiction, focused on human relationships and the growth of the individual. It is educational, sometimes to the point of didacticism. The stories Canfield had told Jimmy and Sally were farfetched, even farcical, their interest centering not on character development but on unexpected twists of plot. They were not educational. They did not have morals either; Jimmy had already developed an aversion to the conventional moral tale. The severely proscriptive "Recipe of a Little Boy of Ten" that appears on the first page of the book makes this clear:

> "I do hate fairies in stories," said Jimmy; "they're so foolish. And I hate things that couldn't possibly have happened. And I despise a story that tries to teach you something without your knowing it. And all that's why I like Mother's stories. But the thing I like best of all about them is that there isn't ever any moral to them."
>
> "No, nor any sense," said a grown-up.
>
> "Yes," said Jimmy, "that is another nice thing about them."

To appreciate Jimmy's "Recipe," one must recall the low status and poor quality of most children's literature in the 1920s. As John Rowe Townsend declares in *Written for Children*, the decade following World War I "was the dreariest since at least the middle of the nineteenth century" (127). I would push the comparison even further back; the period between 1840 and 1860 was one of lively experimentation in children's literature, while the 1920s provided mainly a rehash of old standbys and a proliferation of formula fiction.[5] Fantasy tended to the light and whimsical, and was dominated by frilly fairies of the Rose Fyleman school; no wonder Jimmy had developed a distaste for "things that couldn't possibly have happened."[6] Good realistic

Made-to-Order Stories was strikingly illustrated in black and white by Dorothy Lathrop. Ironically, Lathrop was known for her pictures of fairies—which Jimmy particularly disliked, as he points out in the "Recipe of a Little Boy of Ten" (p. 1). The illustration accompanying the "Recipe," however, gives the artist the last word, and adds yet another layer to this multi-layered book. Copyright 1925 by Harcourt Brace & Company, renewed 1953 by Dorothy Canfield Fisher. Reproduced by permission of the publisher.

Dorothy Lathrop designed an individual headpiece for each of the stories in the book, incorporating the list of objects the story would contain. The headpiece for "The Angry Polar Bear" (p. 25) includes a dog, some sand, a little boy, an elephant, some water, and a polar bear, while the headpiece for "The Father's Story" (p. 169) includes a hot water bottle, a tub of lard, a wild bull, a hunk of chewing gum, and a barrel of lime-sulphur solution. The challenge—which she clearly enjoyed—was to combine such extreme incongruities into a visually satisfying design. Copyright 1925 by Harcourt Brace & Company, renewed 1953 by Dorothy Canfield Fisher. Reproduced by permission of the publisher.

fiction for older children was extremely rare. The old-fashioned moral tales were still around, and Lucy Sprague Mitchell had recently published the *Here and Now Story Book* (1921); Jimmy seems to have disliked the imperfectly concealed educational agenda of the new style as much as the predictability of the old. Had he been more than three when his mother wrote *Understood Betsy*, he would probably have seen personally to the elimination of its didactic passages.

"The Angry Polar Bear," a typical made-to-order story, is neither whimsical fantasy nor utilitarian here and now. Like the others, it begins with a framing scene in which the fictional Jimmy stipulates the objects it will contain—in this case, a dog, some sand, a polar bear, an elephant, some water, and a little boy. "'Oh, that one!'" says Jimmy's mother. "'The one about the little boy who lived quite close to the Zoological Garden, so that he used to go and play there, the way you play in our yard'" (25). The leap straight into an interesting and unlikely (but not impossible) situation is also typical.

One by one, the objects are worked into the story. The boy abandons his *sandpile* to play hide-and-seek with his *dog*, and is hiding in a hedge just inside the zoo, when a *polar bear* gets loose. Frightened at first, the boy soon realizes that the bear is simply enjoying his freedom, "sauntering up one path and down another" (28). But of course, the bear has never seen an *elephant* before, let alone an elephant begging with its trunk for peanuts.

The startled bear claws out at the trunk, sending the elephant into a frenzy. "You see he'd been petted and fussed over and cared for so well all his life, that it wasn't just his trunk that was hurt. It was his feelings. . . . He squealed and screamed and tore around his yard, bang-whanging against everything in it, and tossing the loose hay around like a tornado" (33).

Eventually, however, the elephant calms down and begins to think. Then he slowly and deliberately entices the bear closer and closer to his cage, till he can reach out and give the bear's ear a hard tweak with his trunk. And now it is the bear's turn to be angry.

> He stood up on his hind legs, about a mile tall, and roared and yelled at the top of his voice, and reached in through the bars, scrabbling with his forepaws to reach the

elephant, and dancing up and down with his hindpaws. And the more he roared and scrabbled and jumped up and down, the weaker the elephant got with laughing. He had to fan himself with his trunk and ears. For the polar bear just kept it up and kept it up. He was just crazy, you see, and not having any real brains to think with, like the elephant, he couldn't invent any trick to play. All he could do was to glue himself to the bars, and reach in farther, and yell louder, and jump up and down faster. (37–8)

Meantime, the boy slips out of his hiding place to tell the keepers, who easily recapture the distracted escapee.

The story ends with a return to the frame, as Jimmy objects, "'But I said there was to be some water in it.'"

"There was. The pool in the polar bear's cage. While the men were wheeling him back toward it, the little boy took the pail he'd used for playing in the sand, and ran ahead and scooped it full of the water from the pool. He thought he'd like to take it home for a souvenir." (39–40)

"The Angry Polar Bear" certainly contains no moral—no hint of "Good bears stay in their cages"—nor any useful information on polar bears or elephants. Like the rest of the *Made-to-Order Stories*, it appears to be merely an amusing tall tale with a real life setting, whose effect is enhanced by the "matter-of-fact and serious" style in which it is written. Other, more recent examples are *Mr. Popper's Penguins, Homer Price,* and *The Twenty-One Balloons.* But in 1925 such tall tales were all but nonexistent; Dorothy Canfield's stories evolved in a niche left unfilled by either the whimsical tellers of fairy tales or the earnest educationists of here and now.

And at some point, Canfield came to value the stories for more than their ability to amuse Jimmy and Sally. She was not one to tell "a thousand of them, more or less" without trying to understand what they meant to her children, thinking through the implications, and, finally, expressing her conclusions in fiction. Her short story, "The Rainy Day, the Good Mother, and the Brown Suit" (in *Fables for Parents,* published in 1937), must have come as a surprise to readers of her earlier treatises on child-rearing. Here, with self-directed irony, Canfield suggests that the rational approach she had always advocated might sometimes fail to satisfy the needs of the child.

The mother in the story, familiar with the latest books on "child-training," has assembled plenty of creative materials for her children to play with on a rainy day. "But, unlike the children in the books, Caroline and Freddy and little Priscilla had not received these treasures open-mouthed with pleasure, nor had they quietly and happily exercised their creative instinct, leaving their mother free to get on with her work" (*Fables* 3). Instead, Freddy wants to put on his brown suit, which she has just washed and is too damp to wear.

Patiently and reasonably, the mother explains why Freddy cannot wear the suit. But reason seems to have no effect on Freddy; he simply gets more and more frustrated, upsetting the other two as well. Things are at a very uncomfortable impasse— the mother angry and bewildered, the children naughty and miserable—when a college-boy cousin unexpectedly drops in and begins telling the children a silly story about a mouse. The mother, listening while she does the dishes, wonders, "'What do they see in him? That story is nothing but nonsense,'" and then suddenly realizes, "'Why that is just what they like in it'" (*Fables* 11). (Like Jimmy's "'Yes . . . that is another nice thing about them.'")

The nonsense of the mouse story short-circuits the vicious circle of misbehavior and failed communication. Relaxed after hearing the story and acting it out, the children voluntarily tell the college student why Freddy had wanted so much to wear his brown suit—because it has "a holster pocket at the back where he can carry his pretend pistol" (11). The student suggests that they sew on pockets for themselves, and the children cheerfully spend the morning "exercising their creative instinct by sewing on queer pockets in queer places on their clothes" (13). For their chastened mother, the ironic happy ending comes after lunch, when the children invite her to play Uncle-Peter-and-Aunt-Molly-and-the-mouse with them, and let her have the best part— the mouse.

This "fable" helps explain why Canfield was willing to give children the high-spirited fun of *Made-to-Order Stories*. Placed prominently first in the *Fables* collection, like a *caveat* for parents to keep in mind as they read the rest, "The Rainy Day" pinpoints what was missing from the educational systems Canfield had been endorsing since 1912—the wild X-factor of nonsense and humor and pure imagination. What the "good mother" learns may be something Canfield had learned herself from Jimmy and Sally in the years between. Like the student's mouse story—which also belongs in the possible-but-unlikely category—her *Made-to-Order Stories* provide children with an escape from real life pressures and frustrations, a chance to relax mentally and emotionally, and return refreshed.

She herself may have enjoyed the chance to escape from serious, realistic fiction and educational nonfiction into a more carefree creative world, where stories "run off as fast as you can talk." She had just completed an intense and painful novel, *The Home-Maker*, whose writing, says her biographer, "caused Dorothy more mental anguish than any of her earlier novels" (Washington 119–120); as a writer, she too was ready for a vacation.

But escape is not the only valuable aspect of this kind of storytelling. In "The Rainy Day" the student tells the story to the children and then acts it out with them; in turn, the children share the story-game with their mother. The story experience becomes a collaboration of adults and children. In *Made-to-Order Stories*, the collaborative element is incorporated into the story itself. The stories are designed to suit Jimmy's tastes, and he selects the objects that each story must contain. His appearance at the beginning and end of the story and his questions and objections further emphasize his active role. (By way of contrast, although Christopher Robin appears in the frame of *Winnie-the-Pooh*, and even as a character in the stories, his role as listener is passive and receptive.) In "The Rainy Day," the story and the game are separate activities, but in *Made-to-Order Stories* the unusual premise makes the stories themselves a kind of game played by Jimmy and his mother.

The happy ending of "The Rainy Day" shows clearly how collaborative play can strengthen the emotional bond between parents and children. The mother recognizes her children's offer to share the story with her as a gesture of their love. In *Made-to-Order Stories* the emotional bond between Jimmy and his mother is never made explicit; Jimmy, of course, would have hated any touch of Lord Fauntleroy and Dearest. But the conclusion of *Made-to-Order Stories* is very like "The Rainy Day"'s. Midway through the book, Jimmy's mother has failed to finish the story of "The Inventive Father"; for once, she is not inventive enough herself to think up some plausible reason why the Chinese medical student should have fallen into the hole in the little boy's cellar—or how to get him out of it. That Jimmy and his mother are really upset by this says something of how much the stories mean to both of them. But it is Jimmy who comforts *her*: "'I tell you, Mother,'" he says, "'if we ever put the Made-to-Order Stories in a book, we'll leave some blank pages at the end of this one. I bet you a nickel somebody will know how it turned out'" (110).

And "The Very Last Story of All" is Jimmy's own solution. His gift to his mother of his first creation—the completed story— brings the book to a close; it is a perfect image of how children repay the long investment of their parents' love.

The aptness of this conclusion, and the careful preparation for it halfway through, make one begin to suspect some lurking sense in these stories after all. And although there is nothing in the form of a "moral," nothing expressed overtly by either Jimmy's mother or the narrator, a pattern emerges from certain repeated and varied elements in *Made-to-Order Stories*, a kind of hidden structure beneath the deliberate effect of randomness. The stories appear in the following order:

1. "The Pony-Cart"
2. "The Angry Polar Bear"
3. "Anchor House"
4. "The Coal-Scuttle"
5. "Sally's Story"
6. "The Inventive Father"
7. "A Story About Ancestors"
8. "The Upside-Down Moral"
9. "The Father's Story"
10. "Jombatiste and the Forty Devils"

11. "Clover's Story"

12. "The Very Last Story of All"

The first three stories create the primary pattern. Who tells the story? Who listens? Who specifies the objects to be included in the story, and what kinds of objects will they be? In the first three chapters, Jimmy's mother tells the story to Jimmy alone, and Jimmy specifies the objects:

1. "The Pony-Cart": "'I believe I'll have it about a sack of potatoes, a busted bicycle, a fox caught in a trap, a pony-cart, and a house afire. And of course a little boy.'"(3)

2. "The Angry Polar-Bear": "'A dog, and some sand, and a polar-bear and—and an elephant, and some water. . . . And a little boy.'" (25)

3. "Anchor House": "'A little boy and a ship's anchor, and a library full of books and a woodchuck and a spider and a bed and a doorknob.'" (41)

We can see that Jimmy favors a nice mixture of the animate and the inanimate, the romantic and the prosaic. We also notice what item all three lists have conspicuously in common. This me-character reflects the normal egocentricity of a child, and although the little boy is not always the protagonist, Jimmy's mother seems willing, at first, to make him a fixture. But in the fourth story, "The Coal-Scuttle," she begs Jimmy to leave out the little boy "'Just this once!'" and Jimmy settles instead for "'A coal-scuttle and a poplar tree and a cow and a cat'" (61). And while Jimmy asks for the little boy again in the fifth story ("Sally's Story"), it is for the last time; although little boys appear in several of the later stories, they are no longer present by Jimmy's orders.

We might argue that he makes up for this restraint in chapter 10 ("Jombatiste and the Forty Devils"), where his list consists of "'just lots and lots of little boys. Nothing but.'" Yet his mother's response—"'That'll be fine. It's always more fun when there's a gang'" (193)—suggests that she sees this as a different sort of thing. The me-character has become a we-character. Jimmy's desire to imagine himself as part of a gang of friends signals a new, less self-centered phase of development.

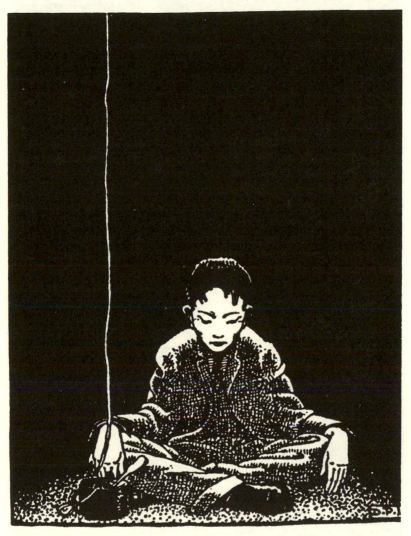

"'But gosh! Mother, you can't leave him there!' shouted Jimmy"(p. 109). The Chinese medical student waits in the cellar for a solution to the unfinished story of "The Inventive Father" in one of Lathrop's most dramatic illustrations. Copyright 1925 by Harcourt Brace & Company, renewed 1953 by Dorothy Canfield Fisher. Reproduced by permission of the publisher.

The little boy sprays the elm tree in Jimmy's inventive solution to "The Inventive Father." Here, Lathrop's use of white space delicately draws our attention to the worms. Copyright 1925 by Harcourt Brace & Company, renewed 1953 by Dorothy Canfield Fisher. Reproduced by permission of the publisher.

This significant difference between Jimmy's first lists and his later ones parallels a change in the teller-listener population. In the first four chapters, the story-game is played only by Jimmy and his mother. An essential feature of egocentric fantasy is to have your mother all to yourself, and this is just what Canfield allows. In chapter 5, "Sally's Story," however, the circle is enlarged. Sally tells the story to Jimmy, their mother, and their grandmother—each of whom contributes something to the initial list of objects. Some of Jimmy's friends join him to hear "The Upside-Down Moral" (chapter 8), and Jimmy's father tells him the story of "Happy-Go-Lucky Henery" (chapter 9). Finally, "Clover's Story" (chapter 11) is told to Jimmy and Clover, a young family friend. Clover even gets to choose the list of objects—false teeth, a pair of tongs, a cricket, and a star—and although Jimmy is a bit reluctant to let her play his role, he gives in and enjoys the story as usual.

It makes sense that "Clover's Story" comes just before "The Very Last Story of All." By relinquishing the privileged yet childish relationship with his mother, Jimmy readies himself for the last step into independence, when he can take her place as problem-solver and storyteller.

Lu Ching, Jimmy explains, was in the cellar by mistake. Attempting to recover his family's stolen ancestral copper bowl, he had confused the little boy's house with an antique dealer's. What's more, it's the little boy (not his mother) who comes up with a solution equally fair to Lu Ching and the dealer. By volunteering for a tree-climbing job that no adult could manage, the boy trades his skill with the antique dealer for Lu Ching's bowl. Years later, several strings of beautiful Chinese beads arrive mysteriously—not for the boy but for his mother, who sells some to buy the refrigerator she has always wanted.

The story's ending parallels what is happening in the telling: while singlehandedly solving the problem of the unfinished story, Jimmy is also giving his mother the gift of his own creation.

These subtly shifting patterns of story content and teller-listener relationship add an element of variation that makes the book less predictable, more interesting. They also trace Jimmy's inner growth from babyhood to maturity. Although he is supposedly ten all along, at the beginning he is self-centered, possessive, and dependent in his relationship with his mother; by the end, he has moved significantly toward independence and a more generous kind of love. Canfield emphasizes this change in Jimmy by limiting the initial teller-listener population to Jimmy and his mother, as though the stories were originally told to him alone. In fact, as we know from her letter to Harcourt, they were told to both children. Although Sally at fifteen might simply have seemed "too old" for the game, Canfield could have fixed this by making both children younger; instead, she chose to move Sally to the periphery, focusing more attention on Jimmy and the evolving mother-child relationship.

Parents who objected to Canfield's philosophy of child-rearing felt that they should be exacting obedience from their children, not "giving in" to them. How could children grow up, if they were constantly indulged and catered to? But Canfield's aim was not to substitute the child's will for hers, but to bypass the whole question of whose will should prevail. *Made-to-Order Stories* reflects this approach. At first glance, it might seem that Jimmy's mother simply gives Jimmy what he wants, stories "made to order." As we have seen, Jimmy is encouraged to be an active rather than a passive participant in the storytelling; his mother allows him to interrupt, as well, and good-humoredly answers his questions or objections. Yet as early as the third story she is already nudging him toward maturity, through a little boy protagonist who makes a hard, grown-up decision.

"Anchor House" begins as a mystery—the boy returns to his room in the middle of the night to find that his bed has disappeared!—but turns into another kind of story when the boy decides to spend the rest of the night outdoors, and rescues a baby woodchuck from a weasel. The boy is sure that he can tame the woodchuck. "He'd be so good to it, it would have to learn to love him!" (56). But after two days, the woodchuck still refuses to eat and will only snarl and glare at him, and the boy realizes at last that it will die unless he returns it to the wild and its own kind. The happy ending of this story is loving something enough to let it go. Emotionally, Jimmy understands and responds. "'I'm glad he let him go,' he said softly" (58). (Though he still wants to know what happened to the bed.) He too will become less possessive in his love for his mother, more willing to share her with others both within and outside the family circle.

By the fourth story, Jimmy's mother is bluntly asking him to leave out the little boy. And the sixth story, "The Inventive Father," pushes him even farther. Her failure to finish it reveals her to be not the all-wise mother goddess that young children naturally believe in, but a fallible fellow human being. Naturally, Jimmy is upset by this. But all his protests— "'But gosh! Mother, you can't *leave* him there!' shouted Jimmy" (109)—cannot make her infallible again. There is even a strong suggestion that Jimmy must accept his own share of responsibility for the disaster. When he comes to ask her for a story,

> It was pouring down rain and Jimmy's mother was taking advantage of it to transplant her phlox. This is a tough, dirty job, and she was muddy to the eyes, and feeling rather grim when Jimmy came skipping down the path like a brownie in oilskins. (95)

She makes clear to him that it is unreasonable to expect a story under these circumstances. Jimmy's innocent self-centeredness is clear too. "'But you don't have to stop your work. You can tell as you plant,'" he says (95); he does, as an afterthought, offer to help her with the phlox! And although his mother finally agrees to tell the story, "she had a feeling from the first that something would go wrong with it" (96). When Jimmy realizes that he will have to finish the story himself, her admission of failure becomes his chance to grow.

Repeatedly, in both fiction and nonfiction, Canfield depicts the unhappy results of parental infallibility. In "The Rainy Day," the mother does at one point think to ask her children *why* Freddy wants to wear his brown suit. What the children hear, however, is not "'What's the matter with the suit he's got on?'" but the parental subtext: "'No matter what Freddy said his reason was, I'd soon show you it was all foolishness'" (*Fables* 5). In *The Home-Maker*, a dominating, "perfect" mother is destroying her own children. Her conviction that she always knows what is best has a withering effect on Henry and Helen of which she is utterly unaware:

> Her tone was reasonable. Her logic was unanswerable.
> Henry shrank to even smaller dimensions as he lay
> helpless on the bed. (40)

Luckily, catastrophe forces her out of the home and into the job
market, where her energy finds a positive direction. What a relief
for Canfield to turn from this relentlessly self-righteous mother
to one who *refrains* from claiming all power and knowledge for
herself![7]

In the end, Jimmy not only achieves something on his
own, but is eager to share his achievement with his mother. As
he tells "The Very Last Story," she in turn adopts his old role,
occasionally interrupting to ask questions. And she accepts his
solution wholeheartedly, with relief and happiness:

> "Well, Jimmy!" she said. "It's almost too good to be true,
> to have it turn out so well, after all our worrying about it."
>
> "Yes, I was glad, too," said Jimmy . . . .
>
> "Look here, Jimmy," she said. "If you can do Made-to-
> Order Stories like that, you won't need me any more. You
> can tell them for yourself now."
>
> For an instant Jimmy looked surprised. Then: "Why, that's
> so!" he said. "I suppose I can." (263)

Like the three children in "The Rainy Day," Jimmy hears
more than his mother's surface words. She is telling him that she
does not want to keep him dependent on her like a baby, that she
is proud to see him capable and self-reliant, and to meet him as
an equal and a friend. She is a Montessori Mother after all.

The frame of *Made-to-Order Stories* expresses Dorothy
Canfield's long-held conviction that the true goal of child-rearing
is to encourage the child to grow freely and confidently toward
maturity. Her objectives within the stories themselves are not
nearly so clear. Except for "Anchor House," they seem to be pure
entertainment, enjoyable nonsense—and we've seen that
Canfield had come to value nonsense simply for its ability to
relax and refresh. Yet the stories are also, in a broad sense,
educational. The basic design of *Made-to-Order Stories* is itself a
play-exercise for the mind and imagination of a child. And their
content, while avoiding morals and messages, suggests the kind
of adults Canfield wanted her children to be.

Like Jimmy, the young reader of *Made-to-Order Stories* is encouraged to take an unusually active role. The reader knows at the outset of each story that certain objects will be included, but not when or how. Watching for them, checking them off mentally as they show up, and spotting the occasional missing object (as Jimmy does in "The Angry Polar Bear") is like solving a kind of narrative puzzle, and Canfield makes the game more challenging by introducing some objects in unlikely or inconspicuous ways. Clover, who is new to it (and a bit sentimental), is miffed when the "cricket" and "star" she has stipulated turn out to be a footstool and a policeman's badge, but Jimmy, a veteran player, is pleased by the ingenuity of the solution.

Complex plots, with events that interlock like a jigsaw in unexpected ways, also stimulate mental activity. "The Coal-Scuttle," though one of the simpler stories, is typical in this narrative technique. A coal-scuttle, bored and feeling sorry for a hungry cat, tells it where veal cutlets are. Maria, the cook, arrives just in time to throw the coal-scuttle at the cat as it streaks down the alley, dragging a cutlet behind it. The flying coal-scuttle is hooked on a wandering heifer's horn, and the terrified heifer stampedes up into the woods. Dislodged at last, the coal-scuttle is picked up by an ex-sailor who has just moved to the country; he finds it very handy for helping himself to a little milk from his neighbors' cows—because who ever heard of carrying milk in a coal-scuttle?

The stories do not open in conventional fashion, either. Jimmy's mother tends to leap into the midst of things, and explain backwards. She begins "The Coal-Scuttle," for example, by wondering aloud "'what would have happened if Maria hadn't lost her temper so'" (62). She goes on to explain that "'it didn't really start with Maria . . . . It started the night before, when the cat didn't catch the mouse she expected to . . .'" (62). Again, Jimmy has come to take this technique in stride, but we can see in "Clover's Story" how it bewilders Clover:

> "Never mind its being all mixed up to begin with," Jimmy reassured her. "You have to get the hang of the Made-to-Order Stories. This is only the beginning."

"But I haven't heard any beginning yet!" cried Clover.
(223)

For Clover a "beginning" must follow the set patterns with
which she is familiar; already, preconceptions are limiting her
ability to grasp something new.

Another element in the complexity of *Made-to-Order Stories*
is the sheer number and variety of their characters—animals,
inanimate objects with human feelings, men, women, and
children—each with their own point of view. "The Coal-Scuttle"
shifts from the viewpoint of a coal-scuttle to those of a middle-
aged cook, a heifer, the coal-scuttle again, and a crafty ex-sailor
in less than ten pages.

In her use of such characters as heifers and coal-scuttles,
Canfield may have been influenced by the same post-war trend
we see in *Winnie-the-Pooh* and *The Velveteen Rabbit* (1922), and all
through the *Here and Now Story Book*; humanized animal and
inanimate object characters were prevalent just then. The
frequency of adults as main characters, however, was (and still
is) unusual, and lifts the stories clear out of the nursery and into
the real world. Is it in spite of or *because of* Jimmy's clearly
expressed preference for little boys with whom he can identify,
that his mother persuades him to empathize with an ex-sailor,
his own grandfather (in "A Story About Ancestors"), an
unsuccessful farmer (in "The Pony-Cart"), a retired army captain
(in "Sally's Story"), busy housewives (in "The Upside-Down
Moral"), and a nervous old maid (in "Clover's Story")?

Even in stories told from a little boy's point of view, the
boy often learns to appreciate someone else's. In "The Angry
Polar Bear," the boy stops being afraid of the bear "almost right
away," when he realizes that it is simply enjoying its new
freedom (27). In "Anchor House," the boy relinquishes his
dream of a pet woodchuck, when he faces up to how the
woodchuck really feels. The variety of viewpoints and characters
in these stories thus adds more to them than further interest and
complexity. In real life, Dorothy Canfield took Sally and Jimmy
to war-torn France with her, rather than leave them behind in
safe, insular America. In *Made-to-Order Stories*, too, she opened
doors to a wider, more adult world and suggested that everyone
out there is as human as we are.

Independence and self-reliance were high on Canfield's list of values for children; her characterization in *Made-to-Order Stories* suggests that she wanted them to grow up thoughtful and tolerant as well, aware of a commonality of feeling that links woodchucks and little boys, housewives and polar bears. Along with this goes a strong New England sense of responsibility. In *Understood Betsy*, Betsy proves her new maturity by taking care of Molly, a younger child, rescuing her when she falls into a pit and finding a way to get them both home from the fair. The lighthearted *Made-to-Order Stories* naturally does not stress this quality in the same way, but it is nonetheless there—and particularly in some of the little boys. The boy in "The Angry Polar Bear" sees to the bear's safe recapture. In "Sally's Story" the little boy helps the retired army captain pull an escaped pig out of a bog. The boy in "Anchor House" learns painfully about the responsibility of those with power. Two of the tales, "The Father's Story" and "A Story About Ancestors," are both about getting somewhere on time, however difficult it may be. An unspoken assumption in all these stories is that when there is trouble, one should try to help.

And yet, co-existing with the emphasis on responsibility (and rather surprisingly for those who know *Understood Betsy*), is an even stronger emphasis on the value of personal freedom— freedom from the conventional thinking of society, from the habits of one's life, from the rigidity of one's own mind. I've suggested that Canfield may have discovered for herself the value of escape through nonsense, and found the writing of these tall tales a liberation from the serious, realistic work she had always done. But liberation pervades content as well as form. Not only does the polar bear escape from his dull cage— so, in their own ways, do the pony-cart, and the coal-scuttle, and Happy-Go-Lucky Henery, a little old car who "was a gypsy at heart" (172). "A Story About Ancestors" begins with Jimmy and his mother escaping from an unwelcome visitor to the woods, where the story can be told in peace. "Jombatiste and the Forty Devils" is about the wonderful holiday that the "lots and lots of little boys" have together. And "The Upside-Down Moral" is about an escaped canary; the point of the story— "'It's the opposite of a moral!'" says the delighted Jimmy (168)—is that the assorted people trying to recapture it, the housewives who have left their spring cleaning and the farmer who abandons his plowing and the Negro handyman who stops rolling the tennis court, all end up enjoying their unplanned holiday in the country. Escape is everywhere in these stories—and it's good.

The psychological analogue to this sense of freedom is a kind of mental flexibility. Observing and judging for oneself. Accepting and adapting to and enjoying the unexpected. Again, the content of *Made-to-Order Stories* recapitulates their form. The twists and turns, the startling openings, shifting viewpoints, and surprising developments of the stories encourage flexibility in the young listener; we can see the results of this regular exercise in the differing responses of Jimmy and Clover. But mental flexibility is also an asset for the story characters. The real moral (or "opposite of a moral") in "The Angry Polar Bear" is not that the bear should not have escaped from his cage, but that he wasn't flexible enough to handle something as unexpected as an elephant. While the elephant uses his brain to get revenge on the bear, the bear, with a more limited mental capacity, can only get angrier and angrier. The little boy, on the other hand, quickly adapts to the unusual situation, first realizing that he can abandon his scary preconception of polar bears, and later seizing the opportunity for its recapture.

The little boy in "Anchor House" also reacts flexibly to the surprise of having his bed disappear; he decides to make the best of things by going outside to watch the dawn begin and look for wild animals. Faithful Peter and his son in "The Father's Story" use all kinds of ingenuity to get their decrepit motor car home in time for the garden party; Peter, says Jimmy's father approvingly, "was a really resourceful trouble-shooter" (180). Even the ex-sailor in "The Coal-Scuttle" is ingenious in his dishonesty. He has no need for a coal-scuttle—as such—but sees at once how to use it for something else.

When she wrote *Understood Betsy*, Dorothy Canfield was focused on the benefits of treating children more like adults, of allowing them access to the real world instead of coddling them in the nursery. She hadn't stopped believing in those benefits when she wrote *Made-to-Order Stories*, but she seems to have added mental openness and flexibility to her list—qualities

possessed less often by adults than by children. Children are
born adaptable, and tend to stiffen up as they grow older. In
stories like "The Coal-Scuttle" and "The Upside-Down Moral,"
adults who retain a youthful flexibility are clearly the better for
it. While in *Understood Betsy* adults have all the virtues, in *Made-
to-Order Stories*, young readers are encouraged to hold on to
some natural attributes of their own.

The strong pro-adult orientation of *Understood Betsy* is due
in part, I suspect, to a personal reaction against the child-
worship so common in literature around the turn of the century.
Betsy actually reads like a parody of a certain type of sentimental
novel, the type precisely described by Gillian Avery in
"'Remarkable and Winning'": a sensitive young girl with
wonderful eyes (usually an orphan) is taken into a severe and
narrowminded household where her stellar qualities are not (at
first) appreciated, but which she ultimately transforms. *Rebecca of
Sunnybrook Farm* (1903), *Anne of Green Gables* (1908), and
Pollyanna (1913) were highly popular examples. Proud of her
New England heritage, Canfield may well have been affronted
by the stereotypically grim and unimaginative New
Englanders—aunts, especially—portrayed in these novels, as
well as the unrealistic, self-indulgent view of childhood. Her
Betsy, a sensitive, big-eyed little orphan girl, is also sent to a
New England farm, where she expects the worst—but it is she,
not her relatives, who needs to change. The formidable Uncle
Henry, Aunt Abigail, and Cousin Ann soon reveal themselves as
warm and loving people. The little child does not lead them;
they lead her.

In *Understood Betsy*, the omniscient adult narrator still had
all the answers. In *Made-to-Order Stories*, with a crucial ten years
of history behind her, "Jimmy's mother" admits her own
fallibility. She knows when she can't finish the story herself.

Unlike most children's books of the 1920s, *Made-to-Order
Stories* looks forward into the century just begun. Its innovative
play with narrative form and the teller-listener relationship, and
its clean break with outworn conventions of storytelling echo the
experimental quality of the best adult literature of its time. The
old balance of power between adult storyteller and child listener
has shifted, too. Deliberately, Dorothy Canfield empowers the

child, who must solve problems left unsolved by the last generation—her generation, that had led the whole world into war.

Jimmy's completion of "The Inventive Father" is her best, hopeful guess at what the new generation might become. We see that the little boy who is both Jimmy's hero and himself is self-reliant and responsible, setting out at once to recover Lu Ching's copper bowl, without even telling his mother what he is up to. His strategy shows that he is observant and mentally flexible as well. He notices that the elm tree outside the antique shop is infested with worms that are dropping all over the sidewalk, and realizes that with his light weight he can hand-spray a tree no adult could climb; this in turn enables him to bargain successfully with the antique dealer for the bowl. But perhaps the most significant aspect of Jimmy's story is that the relationship with Lu Ching does not end there. Jimmy goes on to tell how Lu Ching

> wrote them lots of nice letters from Cincinnati while he went on learning to be a doctor; and he wrote them lots of nice letters from China, too, and the little boy used to have the most splendiferous stamps to trade off to the other kids. (258)

Eventually, from the messenger who brings them the beads, the boy and his mother learn

> how Lu Ching was head doctor in the hospital in their town, and how he was married and had lots of babies, and one of them was named after the little American boy, and how often he told his children the story about the time he fell into the hole in the cellar. (261)

A Chinaman in the cellar would be a sinister figure for most readers in that very racist decade,[8] but the boy who has learned to empathize with woodchucks, housewives, ex-sailors, coal-scuttles, old maids, polar bears, and his own grandfather can take a Chinaman in his stride. What is strange and alien about Lu Ching simply makes him more interesting to know:

> They had ever such a good time, visiting with Lu Ching, and hearing about China. The little boy had always wondered, for instance, how ever they could manage to

eat green peas with chopsticks, and now he could ask.
(254)

The foreign invader is transformed into a friend, and Lu Ching takes back to China not only the scientific training of the West, but lifelong friendship with an American family. "The Very Last Story of All" suggests, both in itself and in the identity of its teller, how a new, open-minded generation might create a more peaceful world. It is an ending that Dorothy Canfield must have enjoyed writing for her son.

She could not have expected that her tall tale might in a sense come true. Yet in real life Jimmy himself went to medical school and became a doctor. He died in World War II, in an attempt to free American prisoners of war from a prison in the Philippines. In their son's memory, the Fishers arranged that the two Philippine doctors who had cared for him be brought to America. "He had told them," Canfield explained in a letter, "just before the attack on the Cabantuan prison began, in which he was mortally wounded, that if they all lived through the desperate undertaking, he would certainly help them come to this country for some post-graduate study. . . . Everybody is being very kind to them at the Harvard Medical School where their presence is regarded (as we regard it) as a sort of living memorial to the Harvard Medical School graduate, who died and is buried in their far Oriental country" (Washington 212–3).

It is hard to read this and not remember that other medical student from a far Oriental country, who named one of his children "after the little American boy."

NOTES

1. Dorothy Canfield Fisher consistently published her fictional works under her maiden name (Dorothy Canfield) and her nonfiction as Dorothy Canfield Fisher. Since I deal here primarily with a work of fiction, I will be using her maiden name throughout the essay.

2. *Books in Print* lists current hardcover editions published by Buccaneer (1981) and Harmony Raine (1980), and a paperback edition published by Dell Yearling (1987).

3. "Jimmy's 'Made-to-Order Stories'" was published in *St. Nicholas* 52, 2 (Dec. 1924). It consisted of three stories: "Anchor House," "Sally's Story," and "The Angry Polar Bear." "Father's Story" then appeared in Volume 52, 3 (Jan. 1925) and "A Story About Ancestors" in Volume 52, 4 (Feb. 1925). In the book, the stories are ordered quite differently, which suggests that Dorothy Canfield gave careful thought to this aspect of *Made-to-Order Stories*. Another significant difference occurs in the frame. Canfield used an "I" narrator in "Jimmy's 'Made-to-Order Stories,'" This gave way by "A Story About Ancestors" to the "Jimmy's mother" she would use in the completed book, creating some fictional distance between herself and the characters.

Canfield had previously published "The Upside-Down Moral" in somewhat different form as "For 'Maginative People Only" in *St. Nicholas* 39, 8 (June 1912). At this point in its evolution, it is not a made-to-order story, but a straightforward, first person narrative purporting to have happened to the Fishers themselves. (Perhaps it really did.) Jimmy is called "Pete" and Sally "Sallie." And Canfield as narrator has not yet found her voice as a children's writer; she sounds ill-at-ease and "talks down" to her audience.

4. Later, she contributed stories for children to a collaboration with her friend Sarah Cleghorn called *Nothing Ever Happens and How It Does* (1940). She also compiled a storyteller's collection for parents, *Tell Me a Story* (1940), and wrote four nonfiction books for young people: *Paul Revere and the Minute Men* (1950), *Our Independence and the Constitution* (1950) (these being the first two books in the famous Landmark series), *A Fair World for All* (1952) at the request of the United Nations, and a book of biographical sketches of great Americans, *And Long Remember* (1959), left unfinished at her death. See Washington 219–22.

5. Picture books and stories of foreign lands appear to have been the only genres characterized by creative innovation and high quality during the 1920s. This was also the decade when mystery stories made their way out of pulp fiction into the mainstream, but these (with the exception of *Emil and the Detectives*, in 1929) were a mediocre lot. Between 1840 and 1860, on the other hand, entire genres of children's literature came into being: the historical novel (with Harriet Martineau's *The Settlers at Home* in 1841 and Frederick Marryat's *The Children of the New Forest* in 1847, followed by Charlotte Yonge in the 1850s), the school story for boys (Harriet Martineau's *The Crofton Boys* in 1841, Thomas Hughes' *Tom Brown's Schooldays* in 1857), and the full-length family

story for older girls (with Susan Warner's *The Wide, Wide World* in 1850 and Charlotte Yonge's *The Daisy Chain* in 1856). There were also major developments in the adventure story and in fantasy.

6. "The appetite for fairies seemed insatiable," writes Gillian Avery, who has analyzed the fairy literature of this period in "The Quest for Fairyland." The few fantasies that have survived from the 1920s—the Pooh books, the Doctor Dolittle series, Eleanor Farjeon's fairy tales, *The Velveteen Rabbit*, *The Midnight Folk*, *Rootabaga Stories*— give a more positive impression of the period than it deserves.

7. The dangerous imbalance of power in the parent-child relationship is one of the themes woven through *The Home-Maker*. Lester, the children's father, becomes conscious of it, articulating a horror that must have been Canfield's own:

> Lester said to himself, shivering, "What a ghastly thing to have sensitive, helpless human beings absolutely in the power of other human beings! Absolute, unquestioned power! Nobody can stand that. It's cold poison. How many wardens of prisons are driven sadistically mad with it!"
>
> He recoiled from it with terror. "You have to be a superman to be equal to it."
>
> In the silent room he heard it echoing solemnly, "That's what it is to be a parent."
>
> He had been a parent for thirteen years before he thought of it. (175)

8. Readers of the 1920s would probably have associated a Chinaman in the cellar with Dr. Fu Manchu, who could often be found plotting the overthrow of the West in abandoned warehouses and other dark places. Sax Rohmer's *The Insidious Dr. Fu Manchu*, the first of this popular series, was published in 1913.

WORKS CITED

Avery, Gillian. "The Quest for Fairyland." *Quarterly Journal of the Library of Congress* 38,4 (1981): 220–27.

————. "'Remarkable and Winning': A Hundred Years of American Heroines." *The Lion and the Unicorn* 13, 1 (1989): 7–20.

Canfield, Dorothy. *Fables for Parents*. New York: Harcourt, Brace, 1937.

————. "For 'Maginative People Only." *St. Nicholas* 39, 8 (June 1912): 675–83.

————. *The Home-Maker*. New York: Harcourt, Brace, 1924.

————. "Jimmy's 'Made-to-Order Stories.'" *St. Nicholas* 52, 2–4 (December 1924–February 1925): 115–27.

————. *Made-to-Order Stories*. New York: Harcourt, Brace, 1925.

————. *Understood Betsy*. New York: Grosset and Dunlap, n.d. [1917].

Fisher, Dorothy Canfield. *Mothers and Children*. New York: Henry Holt, 1914.

Romalov, Nancy Tillman. "Progressive Education: Two Comparative Views." *The Lion and the Unicorn* 12, 1 (1988): 141–6.

Washington, Ida H. *Dorothy Canfield Fisher: A Biography*. Shelburne, Vermont: New England Press, 1982.

American Mosaic: Florence Crannell Means

> Quite as vivid as the past . . . is the present with its
> varicolored racial groups, aboriginal and imported; and,
> shifting kaleidoscopically across the pattern of brights and
> darks, the continual trek of our migrant workers. It's since
> I've grown acquainted with the children of one after
> another of these groups that I've begun to harbor a deep
> desire: to fix this mosaic of American youth between
> booklids, one motif at a time.
>
> Florence Crannell Means, *"Mosaic"*

Florence Crannell Means, often looked at askance in her own time, might be equally controversial today. In the 1930s and 40s she became a specialist, all but unique, in ethnic literature for the young. Her heroines were black, Latino, Hopi, Navajo, Japanese-American. Her novels won high praise from contemporary reviewers; one was a Newbery Runner-up in 1946. But on what grounds might we want to revive them? Now that we have writers for children who are themselves black, Latino, American Indian, and Japanese-American, why rediscover this white author, most of whose books were written forty, even fifty years ago?

From a historical standpoint, certainly, she should be better known, for she was a pioneer in an area of children's literature that has assumed major importance in our own time. Before World War II, with very rare exceptions, ethnic and religious minorities were represented in American children's books only in rigidly defined and usually demeaning supporting roles. Blacks were servants, usually comic servants; black children were comic playfellows. American Indians were pitiful drunks or ruthless enemies. The list of the Newbery Award winners and runners-up from 1922 to 1945 includes stories set in China, India, South America, Hungary, Poland, Bulgaria, and Japan, but small evidence of America's own ethnic variety. (*Waterless Mountain* by Laura Adams Armer, with its Navajo protagonist, is the one prominent exception.) As late as the 1940s, books like *Daniel Boone* (1939) and *The Matchlock Gun* (1941), which promote the American Indian stereotype at its most violent and negative, received the highest accolade of the American Library Association. Against this background, Means's unabashed delight in the American mosaic and her desire to picture it in books for young people seems truly remarkable.[1]

Three strong influences set her on the path: her religious faith, family support for her creative work, and a first-hand acquaintance, from childhood onward, with a wide variety of cultures and races. Her father was a Baptist minister, a scholar and poet. According to Siri Andrews, Means's earliest memories were of "the men and women of many races who visited in their home"; "to her a mingling of people of different colors on an equal footing has never seemed strange" (3). In *The Junior Book of Authors* Means herself tells us that she dreamed in childhood of being a missionary, an artist, a kindergarten teacher, and a writer—and that her parents, in a household where "books came before clothes," were ready to encourage any or all of these ambitions. Later encouragement was supplied by her lawyer husband. "His intense delight in literature and all the arts has made him enjoy my writing as keenly as I," she says, "and he has always helped 'make time' for my work, invariably voting for a poem in place of a pie. Honestly!" (Kunitz 254). Her daughter Eleanor, too, and her daughter's friends, provided both inspiration and audience. And Denver, Colorado, where the Meanses settled, proved to be home to an intriguing mixture of racial groups. It had its own black community, and Eleanor's Camp Fire group included Latinos and Japanese-Americans (Andrews 21). In the late 1920s, Means widened her scope, visiting the mission schools of the Southwest; here she grew to know both Hopi and Navajo well enough to make lasting friends among them, even acquiring a small Hopi namesake, Florence Means Lahpo (Andrews 18).

Her earliest novels, *Candle in the Mist* (1931) and *Ranch and Ring* (1932), belonged to an already-established genre, the pioneer story based on family memories—in this case, her mother's. Like Laura Ingalls, Means's heroine Janey Grant struggles with blizzards, grasshoppers, and a prairie fire, and begins teaching at fifteen. But we miss the emotional depth and intensity, the complex characterization, and the symbolic structuring that make parallel episodes so compelling in the Little House books. A lost treasure and a missing heir supply a more contrived and superficial excitement to Janey's story.

From the pioneer past, Means moved into the contemporary world, now drawing on Eleanor's experiences and her own. Here her crusading spirit found more room for action. *Dusky Day* (1933) and its sequel *The Singing Wood* (1937) are lighthearted tales of college life in southern California based on Eleanor's undergraduate years, while *Penny for Luck* (1935) is one of those many stories of a little orphan girl who finds a family. But a central theme of all three books is the need to accept and understand differences in upbringing and social class. Dusky, unconsciously snobbish, learns to tolerate and even admire her three suitemates, girls from homes radically unlike hers. Penny's new family has to see through her illiteracy, her uncouth speech and ways, to the loyal, loving child underneath. By 1937 and *The Singing Wood*, Dusky's fondness for a little Mexican girl has broadened to include Carmelita's whole family, and a serious interest in Mexican culture. There is even a black student at her college, the realistically wary Cordelia, with whom she finally succeeds in making friends.

Already evident in these novels is Means's painstaking authenticity, later a key asset of her ethnic fiction, which creates an unusually strong sense of time and place. *Penny for Luck* is one of the few children's books of its decade in which the Depression is not incidental but a constant and inescapable reality. And when we read *Dusky Day*, we know that this is exactly how an artistic college girl would decorate a suite in 1933:

> Dusky had suggested side curtains of black glazed
> chintz and glass curtains of sun-yellow voile, and Mary
> Beth and Joan had agreed, after a surprised hesitation.
> Only Maxine had held out for frilly pink and blue.
>
> "Why, you're nerts!" she had flung at them . . . . "And
> what am I to do with my budwar pillows if you use that
> yellow and black stuff, I ask you?"
>
> "We'll all have to do something with our boudoir
> pillows," Dusky reminded her, staring arrogantly down
> her nose at Maxine's sulky little face. "Some of them will
> be darling covered in—in black oilcloth with yellow
> flowers appliquéed on. And yellow gingham with black
> silhouettes." (41)

Yellow gingham with black silhouettes—of course!

Around the same time, Means began a series of books for younger children for the Christian Friendship Press, simple stories with the overall theme of Christian ethics in a multi-ethnic democracy. *Rafael and Consuelo* (1929) was about Mexican immigrants, *Children of the Great Spirit* (1932) about American Indians, *Rainbow Bridge* (1934) about a Japanese-American family. Later she would add *Across the Fruited Plain* (1940) about migrant workers, the equally timely *Children of the Promise* (1941) about Jewish children in a multi-ethnic neighborhood, and *Peter of the Mesa* (1944) about Hopi Indians. These openly didactic tales were her initial venture into what would become her special territory. Then in 1936, for the first time, she combined her interest in American minorities with the complex characterization and richly detailed style of her novels for teenagers in *Tangled Waters*, the story of a Navajo girl seeking her own compromise between old ways and new.

By 1940 Means was able to clarify the vision that unified her work in "Mosaic," written for *The Horn Book*. Her aim was no longer simply didactic; the sheer variety and beauty of American ethnicity appealed to her for its own sake. Yet she was also hopeful of being able to work for better understanding between ethnic groups through her stories for teenaged girls:

> Wouldn't it change something if Rabbit-Girl, Willie-Lou, O
> Mitsu San, Priscilla, were to understand each other better?

> If Priscilla could see why some of these are backward and
> slow of adjustment? What gifts each has for all? (35)

If "backward and slow of adjustment" strikes a condescending note for us, the phrase "What gifts each has for all" suggests that Means was not advocating a culturally homogenized society. The tesserae in a mosaic retain their own bright individuality. And we should keep in mind that the Priscilla of 1940 was far less informed about minority problems than she is today. She would not have realized that adverse living conditions and social handicaps, rather than innate inferiority, held Navajos, blacks, and Latinos at the poverty level of her society. And she was Means's primary audience. While Means hoped to be read by girls of other groups as well—by Rabbit-Girl and Willie-Lou and O Mitsu San—she knew, realistically, that Priscilla was most likely to have the necessary reading ability and leisure time. And it was Priscilla who needed to know, most urgently, about cultures other than her own.

The written mosaic is impressive. It extends from the 1930s to the 1960s, including stories with black heroines (*Shuttered Windows, Great Day in the Morning, Reach for a Star, Tolliver*), stories about Indians of the Southwest (*Tangled Waters, Shadow over Wide Ruin, Whispering Girl, Our Cup Is Broken*), about Japanese-Americans (*The Moved-Outers*), about migrant workers (*Knock at the Door, Emmy*), and about Latinos (*Alicia, The House under the Hill, Teresita of the Valley*). Not all are of high quality. Like many popular writers for children, Means was over-prolific, sometimes repetitive and sometimes hasty. Her old dependence on implausible coincidence and predictable varieties of suspense still lingered, weakening more than one plot. Often her desire to teach intruded too obviously.

But she also knew how to engage and entertain the reader: how to make everyday incidents and crises seem as important to us as they are to the characters; how to capture the flavor of a place, a time, or a culture with precise, memorable detail; how to involve the reader with her protagonist. Priscilla must have been startled more than once to find herself identifying with a girl from some ethnic group she had been brought up to despise.

Of all Means's ethnic novels, two in particular retain their ability to catch the reader by surprise, even after fifty years: *Shuttered Windows* (1938) and *The Moved-Outers* (1945).

Shuttered Windows grew out of a visit to the Mather school for black girls in South Carolina. Means originally had no intention of setting a novel there. In fact, she tells us, she found its students "so sensitive, so race-conscious" that she deliberately kept "authorship in the background lest they think themselves copy" ("Mosaic" 39). But on the last evening of her visit, a group of girls gathered to talk with her.

> They talk of hopes and plans, and, only a little, of the suffering and humiliation that come from being born brown. And abruptly, as if by prearrangement, two exchange glances and one says, "We-all wish you'd write a book about us, M'm. *Like we were white girls.*" ("Mosaic" 39–40)

Means repaid that moment of trust to the fullest of her ability. She settled in at Mather, to absorb the setting as she wrote. Aware of the limitations of her own viewpoint, she read the book aloud, chapter by chapter, to two senior English classes, revising according to their suggestions (Andrews 20). Wisely, too, she made her black protagonist a Northern girl from Minneapolis, for whom Mather is very nearly as alien an environment as it was to Means herself. Harriet's bewilderment, her alternating fascination and dismay, her gradual initiation into a new culture are entirely convincing, and draw the reader in with her.

As the story opens, Harriet Freeman is traveling to Gentlemen's Island off the South Carolina coast to meet her great-grandmother, her only living relative. In order to stay near Granny, she reluctantly enters Landers School (Mather), which seems to her much inferior to the integrated high school she had attended in Minneapolis. At first, she remains proudly aloof, finding little in common with the other students, and is thoroughly resented in return. But she grows fond of her timid little roommate, Mossie Clapp, and begins to appreciate the handicaps that girls like Mossie must struggle to overcome. Her carefully hidden musical and athletic abilities come to light; she joins the basketball team, and plays the piano for a school festival. Gradually, she becomes a part of the community and makes valued friendships there.

Gradually, too, her respect for Richie Corwin, a young islander ambitious to help his people, turns toward love. At first she encourages Richie to leave the South and "make something of himself." But by the end of the book, southern blacks have become "my people" for Harriet as well. She gives up her plans to study music in favor of becoming a teacher, and resolves to work with Richie to raise living standards on the island. *Shuttered Windows* has none of the implausible plot contrivances that mar several of Means's novels. Harriet's change of heart is the result of no single dramatic incident, but of her own inner growth.

The two main settings—the island and the school—are vividly presented, the lush loveliness of the island contrasting with the Spartan dormitories and classrooms of Landers. In her youth, Means had dreamed of being an artist and attended art school for two years; her eye for color and visual detail, her sensory awareness, and her ability to see beauty in an unconventional context are among her strongest assets as a writer. With Harriet the reader feels the slumberous heat of the island, hears its sounds of "sea and wind and birds" (26), sees "the deep dust of the back yard . . . patterned like an engraved tablet by the feet of Granny's motley crew of hens" (23), tastes Granny's crisp, nutty hoecake, with a savory mixture of rice and beans "seasoned with slivers of red chili and hot from the kettle" (44). Even the stationery on which Richie writes to her has its distinctive smell— "stationery that had evidently aged in a village store: it held definite flavors of tobacco and drugs and dried fish and perfume and kerosene" (4).

Means writes with appreciation for the island culture, its rich traditions of hospitality, celebration, and worship. Even "Negro dialect," used commonly in this period as an indicator of black ignorance and inferiority, is presented positively; Harriet finds the Gullah dialect of the islands "as lovely as French patois" (9).[2] Where the stereotypical southern black was invariably shown living in a state of squalor, Means depicts the island homes as clean and attractive, despite their poverty.

Expecting the worst, Harriet is pleasantly surprised by Granny's cabin:

> Its walls and ceiling, its doors and shutters, were tidily papered with fresh magazine and newspaper pages. The doors and windows were curtained with white cheesecloth, which blew out lazily because there was no glass. The uneven floor was gay with rag rugs, and a neatly quilt-covered bed filled a quarter of the floorspace. (22)

Landers, on the other hand, has a "musty, salt-sweet odor" (12) and mold and mosquitoes and silverfish and bare board walls.

> "You've probably noticed that none of our walls are papered," Miss Francis observed cheerfully. "It's too damp here: paper peels off at once." (12)

The charm of Landers lies in the incidents and customs of school life, and Means is as deft as she was in *Dusky Day* at making the reader feel part of them—the swimming expedition, the kitchen-painting project, study hour in the library, the basketball game at Booker, the stacking of Harriet's room by her enemy Willie Lou, clothes and hair-straightening and the dolls that decorate the girls' beds—and the sheer variety of girls who live there together.

Characterization is another noteworthy aspect of *Shuttered Windows*. Means is impressively in advance of her time, not simply because her heroine is black, but because Harriet is also strong, proud, and beautiful—and in ways that reflect not only her individuality but her racial heritage. From the beginning, she is linked with her great ancestor, Black Moses, and the word "handsome" is used to describe them both:

> With what satisfaction he would have regarded this descendant of his, whose head was unbowed in the land of his captivity! Harriet was as handsome as he could have been: a bronze maiden, eyes straight-gazing under brows that frowned with thought; hair cloudy black; full lips well cut; smooth, brown skin stained with dusky red. (6)

Means musters her verbal resources to find phrases that evoke beauty while forcing us to recognize that the beauty is not

Harriet, the heroine of *Shuttered Windows*—proud, black, and beautiful.
Illustration by Armstrong Sperry from *Shuttered Windows* by Florence
Crannell Means. Copyright 1938, © renewed 1966 by Florence Crannell
Means. Reprinted by permission of Houghton Mifflin Co. All rights re-
served.

Armstrong Sperry was also the author-illustrator of many stories based on his own travels in the South Pacific, including the 1941 Newbery Award winner, *Call It Courage*. His portrait of Harriet's "Granny" is remarkable not only for its ethnological accuracy, but for the strength, dignity, and beauty it reveals in its subject. Illustration by Armstrong Sperry from *Shuttered Windows* by Florence Crannell Means. Copyright 1938, © renewed 1966 by Florence Crannell Means. Reprinted by permission of Houghton Mifflin Co. All rights reserved.

Caucasian but African. She was fortunate in her illustrator, Armstrong Sperry, whose striking portraits of Harriet, Richie, and Granny are as far from the usual grinning caricatures as one can imagine.

Harriet's strength and pride also reflect those of her ancestor:

> Even when she was small, her father had said . . . "Mark my word, she gets her height from Grandpa Moses; those broad little old shoulders, too, and the uppity way she flings back her head." (3)

The deliberate choice of "uppity," traditionally a danger word when applied by whites to a black man, is especially significant. Black Moses, Harriet eventually learns, was flogged to death for teaching his fellow slaves to read and write. "'I thought you'd be shamed,'" says Richie. "'Y'all thought he was king-proud—Black Moses—and him flogged like a horse'" (206). But far from feeling shame, she glows with a deeper pride; her discovery of the manner of his death is what finally triggers her choice of a career. "'If Black Moses could die for my people, I guess I can work for them,'" she says (206). Even one of Harriet's white teachers expresses her admiration for Black Moses, calling him "'a nobleman'" (159).

As she talked with the students at Mather School, Means must have sensed their need to find pride in their racial heritage. Through the characters of Harriet and Black Moses, she suggests—a remarkable suggestion for the 1930s—that such pride is not only valid but necessary for black Americans to progress as a people.

The characters of Richie and Granny reinforce this theme. Richie, too, is handsome, and a natural leader—though it must be admitted that Harriet dominates him effortlessly! He and Granny show how dignity, kindness, and intelligence can co-exist with poor grammar—even, in Granny's case, illiteracy—and naive ignorance of the outside world. Knowing them helps Harriet get past her own prejudices. In the beginning, she feels a "sick shame" (26) when she learns that Granny cannot read. But she is also struck with admiration for her great-grandmother, seeing her as "an Ethiopian princess" (23), and "as stately and beautiful as an old woman could be" (26).

Granny, in a patched calico dress and a white kerchief and
apron and headcloth. Granny, whose old face was like
those of proud bronze statues Harriet had seen: high,
carven nose flaring strongly at the nostrils; eyes deep-
socketed; cheek planes flat; mouth long and cleanly cut,
flexible for speech and laughter, firm for closure. Granny,
fit child of Moses. (23)

Granny, too, is linked with the noble heritage of Black Moses.
And later, when Harriet hears the moving story of how Granny's
strength and courage saved the life of her small grandson—
Harriet's father—in the terrible hurricane of 1893, her
admiration, and the reader's, grows.

Means knew better, however, than to substitute a new
stereotype, however appealing, for the cringing subservience
and jollitude of fictional Mammys and Sambos. Not all African-
Americans could be strong, proud, and handsome. One point
that she drives home consistently throughout her ethnic fiction is
the variety of personality and character within any ethnic
group.[3] In *Shuttered Windows*, the student body of Landers
provides an effective demonstration, with its full range of
backgrounds, temperaments, and personalities. As Harriet
surveys the dining room at her first meal, looking for girls who
attract her, she picks out

a serious little dumpling with wide-set eyes and pretty
manners; a willowy girl with a beautiful, tragic face; a
large-framed, kindly one who made her think of a young
edition of Granny; an arrogant one, modishly dressed,
who regarded the scene coldly, under drooped lids. (64)

Her chosen companions are a study in contrasts: the flip,
sophisticated Johnnie La Rocque from Jamaica and New York
City, and Mossie Clapp of Green Corners, the little country girl
whose "feeble drawl and hanging lip" remind Harriet
uncomfortably of the film caricature Stepin Fetchit (76). Yet
another memorable character is the tough and hostile Willie Lou,
a civil rights leader born tragically before her time.

We can see flaws in *Shuttered Windows* from our present-
day perspective. That Harriet should encounter so few instances
of Jim Crow segregation or white arrogance in South Carolina
(or even Minnesota) is certainly unrealistic. Dorothy M.

Broderick, in *Image of the Black in Children's Fiction* (1973), further criticizes Means for not allowing Harriet "to achieve her stated goals," creating "situations that pressure Harriet into accepting the idea of being a teacher" (80) instead of a concert pianist; she associates Harriet's decision with Booker T. Washington's advocacy of "industrial" rather than "classical" education for African-Americans. In fact, however, Harriet's "stated goal" is to be a composer, not a pianist, nor does she abandon it in the end. "'What I really want is to compose, Richie. . . . You reckon I'd do more if I was in big cities . . . ? No. I'll do bigger things on Gentlemen's'" (204). A fairer criticism is that the majority of black characters seem to accept white injustice almost without protest. True, Harriet is outraged when she encounters schools for black children that meet only four months in the year and are supposed to make do without books, pencils, or paper. "'How can they expect us to rise when we've no more chance than that?'" (190). But she is silenced on hearing that schools for mountain whites are no better, and that the South as a whole is poor. No one suggests the integration of all southern schools—black and white, rich and poor—as a possible solution.

But then, in 1938, no one would have suggested it. For present-day readers, one particularly valuable aspect of *Shuttered Windows* is that it shows so clearly the limited options then available to southern blacks, even young blacks as gifted as Richie and Harriet. Means focused on making the best of these options, rather than trying to change the system. And yet, because she was a sensitive observer, and faithfully transmitted what she saw and heard and felt, *Shuttered Windows* can surprise us with foreshadowings of the social revolution still thirty years down the road.

In 1965 *The Autobiography of Malcolm X* shocked many readers by claiming a new source of pride and solidarity for African-Americans in their Islamic heritage. In *Shuttered Windows*, Harriet solves the mystery of Granny's sunrise ritual:

> She was kneeling before that window in her high-necked, long-sleeved nightgown. . . . While Harriet blinked drowsily, the old woman bowed her grizzled head to the floor, once, twice, three times.

> "La-la-la-la-la!" she intoned as if humming in her deep
> voice; and then, very simply, "Blessed King Jesus, keep
> Yo' chillen safe and good dis day, Amen!" (154)

When Granny shows Harriet and Richie a stool carved by her
father with a strange alphabet, Harriet suddenly guesses the
truth: Black Moses was a Muslim, literate in Arabic. Granny's
bows to the rising sun were once a prostration toward Mecca,
and the ritual chant passed down from Black Moses to his
descendants was the prayer of Islam, "Allah il Allah il Allah."
Despite Means's own strongly Christian beliefs, she presents this
revelation as wholly positive, adding yet another level to
Harriet's appreciation of her great ancestor. For the young reader
of 1938, Harriet's discovery must have opened up a fresh and
very startling perspective on black history.

   Another foreshadowing is Willie Lou's talk in chapel on
"The Uplift of Our Race," with its vehement call for black
solidarity and black pride:

> "We don' have to try to be white folks. We aren't white.
> And colored must be good as white, or why did the Lord
> make 'em . . . ?"
>
> Her voice rose. "Quit lookin' to the white folks, I tell you.
> They don' mind if they did drag us here in the first place.
> They don' mind if they did take us away from our people
> and our country. They think it's fine to spend a couple
> dollars a year to teach a colored child and fifty to teach a
> white—" (86)

And Willie Lou's anger finds a swift response.

> Before Willie Lou had finished speaking, there were
> murmurs and even hisses from various parts of the room.
> The sound was like the wind after the sultry calm that
> precedes the great storm. It was like flame breaking out
> from beneath a blanket of smoke.
>
> Harriet looked around her in astonishment. She had not
> realized that these girls were tinder, ready for the spark, or
> smouldering flames, ready for the breeze. (86)

   Again, it is startling to see such a scene depicted in a novel
of this era, nearly thirty years before "the great storm" of the
Civil Rights Movement finally broke loose. One suspects that the

scene must have been based on one Means actually witnessed or heard described at Mather School. She was also aware of the forces counteracting the potential for violent revolution. In *Shuttered Windows*, the incident is resolved when another student, Hannah (the "young edition of Granny"), speaks out, reminding the girls that their dedicated white teachers are helping them "move up together," and then raising a spiritual, "Great Day!":

> "*They* ain' never done us any harm. *They* don' owe us an education. I'm glad to God for 'em: they're givin' us all they got. If we use it like we ought to, I reckon we march up together, like Willie Lou say."
>
> Without a pause, her deep voice swelled out through the room in the spiritual that Harriet loved best:
>
> "Great Day! The righteous marchin' . . ."
>
> A few at a time, uncertainly, other voices took their answering parts until at length the hundred were gathered in the tide of noble sound. (87)

Means—and Harriet—are clearly on Hannah's side; they find the hostile Willie Lou, and the girls' response to her, alarming. Yet Means does not simply condemn her, either. She concedes that although Willie Lou makes Harriet "see red," she cannot help admiring Willie Lou's "spirit and determination . . . . Willie Lou saw visions and made her companions see them" (100). It is Willie Lou who recognizes the symptoms of racial self-hatred for what they are:

> "Looks like we could have our doll-babies colored. Looks like when we draw pictures of us fo' the school paper we could anyways make us look tanned. No suh! Ev'y one of those gals we draw is lily-white. And ev'y one of them doll-babies is buckruh." (108)

And Harriet can feel "some sympathy" with this; "she had rather admired Willie Lou's round brown little doll, the only dark one she had seen at Landers" (108-9).

Means would live to see the revolutionary fervor of Willie Lou and the Christian faith of Hannah join forces in a "righteous marchin'" that would transform the South forever. In 1963, she would become one of the very few writers to deal with the Civil

Rights Movement in a contemporary novel for young people. Too deeply troubled by the violence it provoked to endorse the Movement wholeheartedly, she was still ready to acknowledge in *Tolliver* how far she had come since *Shuttered Windows*. One of its main characters is a young law student, repeatedly thrown in jail for his participation in sit-ins and Freedom Rides—the son of Harriet and Richie Corwin.[4]

Shuttered Windows opens a window on a corner of the past that is fascinating both for its own sake and in its relationship to later history. Moreover, the novel still succeeds in doing what all of Means's ethnic fiction was primarily designed to do—help girls of one ethnic group to better understanding of another. It is Priscilla, not Willie Lou, who has to be shown that black personalities differ as widely as white, and that an uneducated black is not necessarily a stupid one. It is she, most importantly, who needs to learn from the inside that a black girl is a human being like herself. Harriet is made an attractive character not only so that black girls will enjoy identifying with her, but so that even prejudiced white girls might be seduced into taking on her point of view. Means even delays her description of Harriet until six pages into the story—effectively disguising her race long enough to get Priscilla hooked.

With this in mind, we can see why Means avoids unpleasant confrontations between black and white characters—in part, because she was always reluctant to stir up bad feeling between racial groups, but also lest she break the spell that holds the white reader in Harriet's skin. Only in the final chapters does she risk an interview between Harriet and Mrs. Taliaferro, descendant of the family who owned Black Moses, an interview that is brief, guarded, and polite. Nowhere does Means demand that white readers feel outrage or guilt for the wrongs their race has done. She is willing to let the reader's conscience work on its own.

In *Shuttered Windows* Means's ability to create sympathetic and memorable characters, her keen sense of setting, and her deftness in handling potentially explosive material, coupled with the sense of urgency and emotional involvement provided by the students of Mather School, came together in one of her finest novels. Similar factors were operating when she wrote *The*

Moved-Outers, a story of the internment of Japanese-Americans during World War II which appeared in 1945.

"Without Evasion," an appreciation of *The Moved-Outers* by the adventure novelist Howard Pease, published that January in *The Horn Book*, gives a clear picture of the volatile political climate into which Means's book emerged. Although the internment camps were closing, the war was not yet over. Anti-Japanese feeling was as strong as ever, and many were arguing that the Japanese should never be allowed to return to the Pacific Coast. The farmers' Granges of Oregon and California, several local American Legion posts, Mayor Bowron of Los Angeles, and the Native Sons of the Golden West had lined up with a Seattle farmers' group called the Remember Pearl Harbor League (Pease 14). "The reception accorded *The Moved-Outers*," warned Pease, "will be a test of our own intelligence and our own integrity" (17). In the same issue, Clara E. Breed also praised *The Moved-Outers* in her article "Books That Build Better Racial Attitudes," and commended Means's publisher, Houghton Mifflin, remarking, "that this book can be published while the war in the Pacific is still going on shows a certain amount of courage on the part of the publishers, but their faith will surely be justified" (61). Houghton Mifflin must indeed have been pleased when *The Moved-Outers* received the Child Study Association Award of 1945 for the best book dealing with present-day problems and was Runner-up for the Newbery Award in 1946.

Means knew, of course, how controversial her book was bound to be. Her personal feelings must be carefully controlled, and her facts water-tight. Much of her extensive research took place "on location" at Amache camp near her home in Colorado:

> The Assembly Centers were like a radio program that is past; they were not to be recovered. All I could do to recreate Santa Anita was to read everything possible about it and talk to evacuees who had lived there. One of these had kept a memory book, and she let me keep it a whole summer. . . .
>
> It was comparatively easy to visit Amache, just overnight from Denver by train. Amache, and a number of evacuees, relocated in Denver, gave plenty of material, physical and spiritual. I've been having in my home boys and girls who

> were outwardly gay and normal, and others who were
> quiet and thoughtful, and a very few who were bitter.
> Almost better, I have talked with them in their own
> barrack homes. . . . The social workers at Amache were
> also kind in giving me their ideas of the situation and its
> effects. And a teacher who had had many of the Nisei
> throughout several years of their high school courses, in
> Seattle, sent me sheafs of letters she had received from
> them in camp, many of them very revealing. . . . (Quoted
> in Andrews)

The end result, as Siri Andrews described it in 1946, is
"remarkably restrained, objective, and fair" (20). "There is no
criticism in the book of the decision which caused the
evacuation, or the way in which it was carried out—only a
description of the humanly tragic results" (21). As in *Shuttered
Windows*, Means is too wise to demand remorse from her young
white readers; she simply lets them experience, from the inside,
how internment feels.

The story opens on the weekend of December 7, 1941, with
scenes of sunny suburban happiness, in ironic contrast to the
events soon to come:

> Yet this Friday afternoon was no different from
> countless others in Sue Ohara's eighteen years. She and
> Emily Andrews walked home from high school just as
> they had walked home from kindergarten together. The
> same California sun shone warm on their tanned faces and
> bare knees, the same soft breeze played with the hair that
> hung at their shoulders, Emily's red hair cut and curled
> under to match Sue's black. (1)

Even more markedly than in *Shuttered Windows*, Means
delays the revelation of racial identity, instead emphasizing the
friendship between Sue and Emily and how much they have in
common. For the first thirteen pages, the young reader is
encouraged to accept Sue and Kim as "ordinary" teenagers like
herself, sister and brother in a happy middle-class family, busy
packing Christmas boxes for their big sister Amy, attending
college back east, and their big brother Tad, in the army. Only
after the radio announcement of the bombing of Pearl Harbor

brutally interrupts their Sunday dinner, does Means supply what have just become crucial facts about them:

> Here were she and Kim, American-born; as American as baseball—ice-cream cones—swing music. No, as American as the Stars and Stripes. Here they were, American from their hearts out to their skins. But their skins were not American. Their skins were opaque, their hair was densely black, their eyes were ever so little slanted.
>
> And their names were Sumiko and Kimio. (14)

Theatrical, yes—but it works. (Even Means's illustrator Helen Blair added to the effect, consciously or not, with her ethnically ambiguous cover picture.) If the blunt equation of "American" with a specific kind of skin, hair, and eyes arouses our protest, the events of the following pages bear it out only too well.

Through the experiences of the Ohara family, Means unfolds the full story of evacuation and internment. Father, the hardworking owner of a prosperous nursery, is taken away by the FBI on suspicion of collaboration with the enemy. Sue, Kim, and Mrs. Ohara are sent first to the assembly center at Santa Anita, then to the relocation camp at Amache, where Father finally rejoins them. Tad battles discrimination in the army, while Amy evades it by posing as Hawaiian. As the story ends, early in 1943, Kim and Jiro, Sue's boyfriend, have enlisted in an all-Nisei combat unit, and Sue is leaving the camp to attend college. Yet Means does not allow history to overwhelm story. Sue's romance with Jiro, her parents' prejudice against him, her discovery that she enjoys teaching young children, and her fear that Kim will join a gang anchor the novel in universal teenage concerns.

Sue is a very different type of heroine from Harriet. Harriet needs to be an outstanding individual whom girls of any race can admire—a "fit child of Moses." Sue is an affectionate, well-adjusted extrovert, with average grades and no special talents or ambitions. Her ordinariness makes what happens to her all the more senseless and frightening. But it also prevents the story from becoming too bleak for young readers to enjoy. It is natural for Sue to adapt well to camp life; she even benefits from being forced to think seriously for the first time about her goals and her ideals.

Her brother Kim, on the other hand, is an idealist, sensitive and intelligent; watching him, through Sue's worried eyes, grow cynical and rebellious shows clearly the harm done to such individuals by race prejudice and social injustice. He is a more complex character than Sue, and most authors would have been tempted to make him the protagonist. Means saw, however, that it was Sue who could illustrate most effectively the insidious long-term psychological damage done by the internment, even to the average, the easygoing, and the seemingly well-adapted. Toward the end, Sue herself has become aware of it. She realizes that

> "many of us are growing sick; abnormal; even when it does not show so plainly as in Kim. Tomi, fading to a colorless shadow. Father, doing nothing but sit; not even playing goh any more. I, afraid to step outside this safe imprisonment." (143)

It is at this point that she resolves to go to college, even if she has to do housework to pay her way through. She, at least, may escape in time.

As in all her ethnic novels, Means choreographs a large cast of minor characters to illustrate the variety within a racial minority. She points out, as Sue washes the family clothes at Santa Anita, that Japanese-Americans span a wide range of professions and social classes:

> Here was the woman who lived beyond the Itos, awkwardly washing out delicate bits of lingerie. Here was the peasant type from the stall beyond the Filkinses', clumping across the sloppy floor on getas, wringing heavy garments with accustomed hands. Here was a Doctor of Philosophy, small and merry-eyed, her head done up in a vari-colored silk scarf . . . . (47)

And she counters the stereotypes most Americans accepted in 1945. "'All Japanese are short of stature,'" quotes a boy at Amache, sardonically, as the Oharas seat themselves in the mess hall at what feels to them like children's furniture (92).

Checking *The Moved-Outers* against a recent account for young people of the internment reveals how many aspects of the event Means succeeded in incorporating into her story, as well as what she chose to omit or downplay. In *Behind Barbed Wire: The Imprisonment of Japanese Americans During World War II* (1982), Daniel S. Davis notes how "hours after the attack on Pearl Harbor, FBI agents rounded up prominent members of the Japanese community. . . . People who had been leaders of community organizations or had connections with Japanese diplomats or trading companies were automatically regarded as dangerous and liable for arrest" (8). In *The Moved-Outers*, FBI men arrive soon after the broadcast and search the house; a few weeks later, Father is taken away. His shaken family can only speculate on the reasons:

> Their pastor, Mr. Clemons, suggested that his visit to Japan ten years earlier might have implied too keen an interest in that country. Doctor Andrews wondered whether it was his asking a member of the Japanese consulate to speak at a Rotary meeting. (27)

"Many Japanese Americans at school or on the job the morning after Pearl Harbor were reassured by Caucasian friends," says Davis (20). "'Sue, you mustn't feel too bad about this mess,'" cries one classmate. "'Nobody blames you'" (17). Means is realistic about Sue's reaction, too. "Their very anxiety to reassure her showed that there was need of reassurance. It put them on one side of the line and Kim and her on the other" (18).

Davis emphasizes the large part played by greedy agricultural and business interests and by the press in pushing for the evacuation of all Japanese-Americans from the West Coast. When Father is arrested, the local paper reacts with the headline CORDOVA JAP HAULED TO PRISON and a garbled story about his supposed espionage. Kim comments that "'the paper's had it in for Dad ever since the editor's brother went bust in the florist business here'" (24). When the Oharas are interned, the editor's brother attempts to buy the nursery for a fraction of its true value. The Oharas are more fortunate than most. They don't have to sell their furniture to a secondhand dealer, because their minister offers to store it for them, and Emily's older sister, who has been studying horticulture, volunteers to take over the nursery till they return.

Often minor characters are used to make a point that the main characters could not encompass without strain. Davis mentions, for example, that evacuation was mandatory for anyone with even one Japanese ancestor (47). On her first morning at Santa Anita, Sue is startled to see a blue eye peeping at her through a knothole; later she meets the little boy's redhaired mother, who explains that her husband's father had a Japanese grandmother (48). This great-great grandmother is enough to make blue-eyed Tommy Filkins legally Japanese.

From Davis's account, we can see that Means did downplay the friction within the camps, and the strikes, protests, and riots that occasionally resulted. The embittered Kim is tempted to join a teenaged gang of "zootsuiters," but their violence amounts to no more than smashing a piano and spoiling a party. Clearly, Means wanted to avoid showing Japanese-Americans in a bad light. Present-day readers might also find the fervent patriotism of Sue, Kim, and Jiro hard to swallow. Could any teenaged boy really say, "'I suppose good things are worth suffering for. I mean things like democracy,'" and suggest naming his horse-stall at Santa Anita "Valley Forge" (58)? Would any teenaged girl assent that "all this would be dignified, made bearable, if we could remember to think of it so: as suffering for our country. For America" (58)? But to find these sentiments exaggerated and implausible is to impose the values of the 1990s on the culture of another era. Movies, newsreels, novels, and magazines dating from World War II all tell the same idealistic story. The openly displayed patriotism of *The Moved-Outers* is part of what makes the book a real window into the past; indeed, it is just the kind of thing that a historical novelist of today would probably mishandle or ignore.

While Means minimizes some aspects of the internment, she also includes some aspects that Davis does not mention— small cruelties that nonetheless weigh heavy in the human scale. It was a minor regulation that pets could not be taken to the camps, but it is no minor matter for the Oharas when they have to destroy the little old dog that has been part of their family for fifteen years.

> When they had smoothed the turf neatly over Skippy's
> catafalque, it was as if something more than Skippy were
> buried there. Sue stood up decisively, rubbing at her face
> with her two earth-stained hands.

"After all," she said harshly, "this is childish. We have
bigger things to grieve about. Skippy was—he was only a
dog. I won't cry about him again. I think I am through
crying forever." (36)

Another minor incident is the shattering of a small child's
innocence, when cowboys fire into the evacuee train on its way
to Amache. Her face cut by a fragment of shattered glass, Mary
Kaneko asks her father, "'Daddy, aren't we really people?'" (85).
The question, Means tells us, is based on one asked by a real
Japanese-American child— "Aren't we human beings?"
(Andrews 22).

Means wanted to convey more than information about the
internment; she wanted to confront young readers with its
reality. But accuracy alone cannot activate the imagination.
Means's sensory acuteness and flair for detail were as essential
as her meticulous research, teleporting the reader into the bizarre
worlds of Santa Anita and Amache:

Sue dozed at length, rousing with a start whenever a
searchlight lashed in at the window. Toward morning her
slumber deepened into profound sleep, so that when she
wakened she pushed hard against the unfamiliar
hammocky sag of her cot, refusing to open her eyes,
though daylight shone through her lids.

The noise bewildered her: thudding feet, shrieking beds,
slamming doors, crying of children. She could hear the
clamor of birds, the rattle of palm leaves. She could smell
spicy fragrances. Yes, but battling those aromas was the
unmistakeable edge of horse odor. And on Sue's nose a fly
settled and bit viciously. Her eyes popped open and she
stared up into the bare rafters, where more flies buzzed
and circled. (44)

Means's sense of beauty and her delight in small pleasures
also have an important part to play, providing a balance to her
grim subject matter. For *The Moved-Outers* is not, surprisingly, a
depressing book—not a book to read dutifully, but a book to
enjoy. There is a fascination in the odd details of life at Santa
Anita and Amache, even a kind of pioneer charm in the
challenge of creating a home in such surroundings. Means
describes the furniture Jiro builds from scrap lumber and the

curtains Mrs. Ohara sews from unbleached muslin, appliquéed with designs cut from Sue's old calico skirt. She tells us about Sue's memory book (based on the book she borrowed from an evacuee to help her recreate Santa Anita); about Sue's high school commencement at the racetrack, and the Seabiscuit pin Jiro carves for her; about the chocolate angelfood cake that Emily's family sends them for Easter, pockmarked with holes because it has been searched with long needles for contraband. There are flowers blooming at Santa Anita, and a strange, dry desert beauty in Amache. It was characteristic of Means's hopeful temperament to suggest that in nearly every life there are small pleasures to cherish, and beauty to lift up the heart.[5]

Both *Shuttered Windows* and *The Moved-Outers* are still well worth reading, and not for their historical significance alone. True, there is no substitute for the author who actually belongs to an ethnic group—who knows what it really is to be Japanese-American or black. No one could have been more aware of this than Means herself:

> To be sure, it's dangerous business to try to interpret other peoples. A writer may be reassured when a Sioux college graduate borrows her Sioux stories to tell at a club meeting. Yet the young Sioux's satisfaction with those tales may not mean that they were vitally "true" pictures: the Indian's own memories may well have vitalized empty husks.

> Maybe it matters more to have a young Chinese girl tell you shyly that she loves the American girl in your college stories; or to learn that a Harlem library club has named itself for your red-haired mountain tomboy; that Japanese girls on the Coast have a fondness for your pioneer Americans; and that a little Southern maid likes your Negro heroine. ("Mosaic" 40)

Means saw her role realistically, as the interpreter of one group to another, not of the group to itself. She was like the popularizer who writes about science or history, not for the scientists and historians, who know already and in greater depth what she has to say, but for the general public with little or no knowledge of the field. Herself a member of the white majority, Means knew what assumptions white readers would make about blacks and Japanese-Americans; what deep-seated prejudices must be overcome; what techniques would help Priscilla step into the shoes of Harriet Freeman and Sue Ohara. There is a place, not without honor, for the good popularizer. And there is still a place for writers like Florence Crannell Means.

NOTES

1. World War II, however, was also the period when a significant number of teachers, librarians, and authors for young people attempted to link the war for democracy abroad with the achievement of a truer democracy in America. Among the works published at this time were Doris Gates's sympathetic story of migrant workers, *Blue Willow* (1940) and John R. Tunis's interracial sports stories, *All-American* (1942) and *Keystone Kids* (1943). Pioneering works of ethnic fiction include Chesley Kahmann's *Gypsy Luck* (1937) and the Indian stories of Ann Nolan Clark, beginning with *In My Mother's House* in 1941. By 1945 Clara E. Breed was able to publish a respectable list of "Books That Build Better Racial Attitudes" in *The Horn Book*.

2. For amplification, see my essay "Black Language in American Children's Literature" in *Infant Tongues: The Voice of the Child in Literature*.

3. A typical example is this passage from *Shadow Over Wide Ruin* (Boston: Houghton Mifflin, 1942), in which a white girl named Hepzibah attends a Navajo ceremony, and realizes for the first time that not all Indians look alike:

> Never would she have expected them to look so like folks in Denver. Here was a woman's face the lines of which turned sourly downward, and another with the petulence of a spoiled beauty, and another that combined tenderness and strength, and a girl's face all dawning eagerness and life.
>
> Here was a pompous rich man and here a greedy lazy one and here a self-satisfied handsome youth with darting eyes, and here the beautiful old Wind Singer.
>
> Only, Hepzy thought, in this far hogan there was a higher average of strong, disciplined faces than she

would have found, say, in a Denver horse-car; fewer
that looked fat of soul and body; fewer slack of mind
and jaw. (121)

4. Means's genuine ambivalence about the best strategy for
blacks to pursue characterizes all her novels with black protagonists.
Great Day in the Morning (1946) includes a powerful episode in which
the heroine's roommate is injured in a car crash and dies because an all-
white hospital refuses to admit her; one of the black characters, the
upstanding Major Tolliver, comments, "'Things move—yes, they move,
but too slow'" (146). Yet another equally upstanding black character
suggests that blacks must overcome their handicaps before they can
expect the handicaps to be removed: "'Until we can equal white people
on their own ground, how can we expect equal consideration?'" (93).
The contradictions between these two points of view are never debated,
and the heroine, Lilybelle, is encouraged (by a particularly implausible
series of coincidences) to go selflessly into nursing instead of gaining
status as a teacher.

By 1957, however, and *Reach for a Star*, Means had apparently changed
her stance on vocations once again. This time the heroine is encouraged
by her college counselor to go into teaching, nursing, science, or music
(though not, for some reason, welfare work), and told, "'Every time one
of us takes and holds a post of dignity it helps our whole group'" (44).
Toni ends up, however, as the wife of a minister. Here too, Toni's
painful experiences of segregation are poignantly described, though
there is no suggestion that she should protest against it. Tolly, in
Tolliver, actually becomes an English teacher at Mather, which is now
co-educational.

5. Late in her life, Means published an uncharacteristic novel of
near-despair, *Our Cup Is Broken* (1969), the story of a Hopi Indian girl
who is unable to find acceptance either in the white culture or in her
own. Very typical of its period, the novel shows a continuing
willingness on Means's part to adapt her work to new times, but it is
hard to imagine anyone enjoying it or wanting to identify with its
protagonist. Celia Anderson has written an appreciative analysis of it in
"Florence Crannell Means: Cultural Barriers and Bridges."

WORKS CITED

Anderson, Celia Catlett. "Florence Crannell Means: Cultural Barriers and Bridges." In *Cross-Culturalism in Children's Literature: Selected Papers from the 1987 International Conference of The Children's Literature Association.* Ed. Susan R. Gannon and Ruth Anne Thompson. Pleasantville, New York: Pace University, n.d.

Andrews, Siri. "Florence Crannell Means." Horn Book 22, 1 (January 1946): 10–30.

Breed, Clara E. "Books That Build Better Racial Attitudes." Horn Book 21, 1 (January 1945): 55–61.

Broderick, Dorothy M. *Image of the Black in Children's Fiction.* New York: R.R. Bowker, 1973.

Davis, Daniel S. *Behind Barbed Wire: The Imprisonment of Japanese Americans During World War II.* New York: E.P. Dutton, 1982.

Kunitz, Stanley J., and Howard Haycraft, eds. *The Junior Book of Authors.* 2d ed., rev. New York: H.W. Wilson, 1951.

Means, Florence Crannell. *Dusky Day.* Boston: Houghton Mifflin, 1933.

———. *Great Day in the Morning.* Boston: Houghton Mifflin, 1946.

———. "Mosaic." *Horn Book* 16,1 (January 1940): 35–40.

———. *The Moved-Outers.* Boston: Houghton Mifflin, 1945.

———. *Reach for a Star.* Boston: Houghton Mifflin, 1957.

———. *Shadow Over Wide Ruin.* Boston: Houghton Mifflin, 1942.

———. *Shuttered Windows.* Boston: Houghton Mifflin, 1938.

———. *Tolliver.* Boston: Houghton Mifflin, 1963.

Pease, Howard. "Without Evasion: Some Reflections After Reading Mrs. Means' *The Moved-Outers.*" Horn Book 21, 1 (January 1945): 9–17.

Rahn, Suzanne. "Black Language in American Children's Literature." In *Infant Tongues: The Voice of the Child in Literature.* Ed. by Elizabeth Goodenough, Mark A. Heberle, and Naomi Sokoloff. Detroit: Wayne State University Press, 1994.

Deep Valley Revisited: The Betsy-Tacy Stories of Maud Hart Lovelace

> She and Tacy sat looking down Hill Street while the
> clouds in the sky behind Tacy's house turned pink. Their
> hands met and as always, unfailingly, joined in a loyal
> clasp.
>
> Maud Hart Lovelace, *Heaven to Betsy*

For nearly as long as girls have grown up with Laura Ingalls, they have enjoyed the Betsy-Tacy stories too. Their author, Maud Hart Lovelace, like Laura Ingalls Wilder, was born in the late nineteenth century and spent her teen years in a small midwestern community. She too fictionalized her own childhood and young womanhood in a series that begins with herself, the protagonist, about five years old and ends with her marriage. As in the Little House books, the narrative matures along with her, growing more complex in style and in outlook as she grows older.

These similarities have done no service to the younger series, which has been ignored by the critics and the more selective standard references—dismissed, perhaps, as a sort of poor relation, lacking both the primitive excitement of the Ingalls' struggle to survive and its epic significance. And it's true that frontier days are already history in the Betsy-Tacy stories; the twenty-five years that separate Betsy and Laura have assigned them to different eras. Deep Valley, Minnesota, where Betsy grows up, has telephones and a high school, even a movie theater. She herself belongs to a well-to-do, middle-class, very happy family. She has close and loving friends, an exuberant social life, and support for her talent as a writer; in high school she worries mainly over not being prettier, and attracting the right boys.

The author, seeing herself at the detached distance of over thirty years, takes Betsy's problems seriously, but not nearly as seriously as Betsy does.

> Tacy didn't care about boys, and with Tacy Betsy almost forgot how important they were. But she was in high school now. Would boys start coming to see her, as they came to see Julia? . . .
>
> "I wish I were prettier," she thought, depression, like a sudden fog, invading the room. (*Heaven* 58–9)

Lovelace writes with a gently ironic humor for teenage foibles and with close attention to their clothes, their parties, and their favorite songs. It is not hard to find the whole series pretty frivolous—an opinion likely to be reinforced by Vera Neville's illustrations for the later books. Her drawings are as fluffy as so many meringues; all the boys look cute and all the girls adorable in their ruffled petticoats and pompadours. Naturally, only girls read books like these—"girly-girl" books, we used to call them—and a feminist may be embarrassed at having enjoyed them as a child.

Yet despite the lack of critical recognition, uncounted numbers of girls did enjoy the Betsy-Tacy books. Most girls discovered them on their own; some shared them with friends or passed on the discovery to their daughters. The old copies circulated steadily in and out of libraries, more and more worn around the corners. In 1979 the books were reissued in paperback, without attracting the slightest interest from specialists in children's literature.

Then, in 1990, events took a dramatic turn. In Mankato, Minnesota—the real-life Deep Valley—a handful of women who had loved the books since childhood formed a Betsy-Tacy Society. When they decided to hold their first national conference in 1992, Lovelace's centenary year, the story was picked up by *Victoria* Magazine and given a short column in its July "Events" section. Suddenly, the secret was out. More than three hundred enthusiasts from thirty-four states flocked to the conference in Mankato. Letters poured in to *Victoria*, and to *The*

Betsy-Tacy Society Newsletter. Over and over, they repeated, like a refrain, "I thought I was the only one."

> "I just read of the Betsy-Tacy Society and I can barely contain my excitement! I thought I was the only adult who loved or even knew of Betsy Ray and Tacy Kelly! Ever since I first read the series in fourth grade, Betsy has been my true best friend and faithful companion. Even now, I still read the complete series at least once a year. . . ." (Kim Wise, *Newsletter* 9)

> "I've been an avid Betsy-Tacy reader since I was 8 years old, and I'm now 31! I read the entire set every couple of years, and I really did think 'I was the only one.'" (LeAnn Richard, *Newsletter* 11)

> "I am 54 years old and seriously 'thought I was the only one' in my age group that read and reread these books. . . . I cannot believe there are 'others' and I am so pleased." (Barbara Millard, *Newsletter* 11)

> "At age 29, I still lovingly reread my library-discard copies of Maud Hart Lovelace on a yearly basis!" (Terry Gur, *Newsletter* 9)

> "I'm so thrilled that I'm not the only one who loves the Betsy-Tacy books and have for over 35 years!" (Linda Treap, *Newsletter* 11)

> "My daughter and I always thought we had exclusive rights to Betsy and Tacy." (Patricia Nelson, *Newsletter* 10)

> "I, too, am a HUGE fan! I received a postcard from Maud Hart Lovelace in 1961. I consumed her books—I *was* Betsy. In 1972, while suffering from leukemia, rereading her books gave me great comfort." (Vicki Miller, *Newsletter* 12)

> "I have never identified as strongly with any characters in a book as I did Betsy & Tacy. I am so lucky to have a nine year old daughter to share the books with." (Ellen Grod, *Newsletter* 12).

> "It's great to know that other people are still reading Betsy-Tacy as adults. I thought I was the only one sneaking into the children's section of the library to check out a copy of one of the Betsy-Tacy books. . . . I can't wait to share them with any children I may have, just as my mom did with me and my grandmother with my mom." (Kathy M. Forbes, *Newsletter* 10)

"Finally! My guilty secret can come out—I'm a 27-year-old career woman with strong feminist leanings who adores the Betsy-Tacy books!" (Laura Northern, *Newsletter* 9)

"Although I was devoted to Laura Ingalls and enchanted by Anne Shirley, I don't think there was a character with whom I identified more than Betsy Ray! And yes, I too thought I was the only one!" (Melanie Novak, *Newsletter* 11)

"I find myself reaching for certain books in the series depending upon what's happening in my life. As my wedding approached last October, I pulled out my copy of *Betsy's Wedding* and made sure to read about her wedding day on the morning of mine. As I reviewed her list for a successful married life, it seemed like advice from a dear, old friend. As I write this, my youngest stepdaughter and I are reading *Betsy-Tacy* together. It is her first introduction to the books, and she's a fan already." (Becky Schol, *Newsletter* 12).

Few children's books survive the transition to adulthood, or outlast the generational changes of fifty years. Such letters are convincing evidence that there is more to the Betsy-Tacy stories than superficial charm. I first realized that my own attachment to them was more than an individual aberration in 1989, the year that the Children's Literature Association held its annual conference in Mankato. The conference prospectus featured Maud Hart Lovelace as a local children's author, and offered a tour of "Betsy's" neighborhood. It was the perfect excuse to take another look at the books I had discovered and enjoyed as a child, and my conference paper became the first version of this chapter. Despite being—as far as I knew then—"the only one," I found the stories not only as enjoyable as I remembered, but more substantial than I had suspected—much more than watered down Laura Ingalls Wilder. They had their own strong individuality, their own appeal, and something of their own to say.

The Betsy-Tacy stories have the excellence characteristic of their genre, the historical novel, enabling the reader to enter into the life of another time. They have the rarer ability to evoke happiness that the reader can share. And they have more complexity than their lighthearted surface might suggest.

Concepts of internationalism, maturation, friendship, and individual integrity are interwoven throughout the series, so that each of the later books, especially, becomes a microcosm of the whole.

The series begins with *Betsy-Tacy* (1940), in the year 1897, when both girls are five, and continues through *Betsy-Tacy and Tib* (1941), *Betsy and Tacy Go Over the Big Hill* (1942), and *Betsy and Tacy Go Downtown* (1943). There is a break here after Betsy's twelfth year; then the series picks up again, at a distinctly higher level of maturity, as Betsy enters high school at fourteen. Betsy is a freshman in *Heaven to Betsy* (1945), a sophomore in *Betsy in Spite of Herself* (1946), a junior in *Betsy Was a Junior* (1947), and a senior in *Betsy and Joe* (1948). *Betsy and the Great World* (1952) takes her to Europe after her freshman year in college, where she witnesses the outbreak of World War I. *Betsy's Wedding* (1955) sees her through her first year of marriage to Joe Willard, the young journalist she has admired since they were both fourteen.[1]

As a fifth-grader, I was more attracted to the later books, with their fascinating preview of teenage life. I still find them more interesting to read—more layered and richer in detail. Betsy herself is reflective and self-aware at fourteen, as she could not have been at twelve. She has become a journal keeper, and the occasional quotations from her journal add another strand to the narrative. To represent the series, I've chosen one of these later books—the quintessential *Betsy in Spite of Herself*.

The year is 1907, and Betsy is fifteen, a sophomore in high school; her older sister Julia, an aspiring opera singer, is a senior, and her younger sister Margaret is nine. Betsy belongs to a lively Crowd of girls and boys, but still feels closest to Tacy Kelly, her oldest friend, and Tib Muller, now living in Milwaukee. Betsy begins the school year deeply dissatisfied with herself. She feels immature and childish, and although boys like her as a friend, she wants them to fall madly in love with her as they do with Julia. A Christmas visit to Tib in Milwaukee gives her the chance to "change herself." She creates a new personality which she sees as "Dramatic and Mysterious," and begins spelling her name "Betsye."

Back home, she succeeds in attracting a prestigious junior, Phil Brandish, and goes with him all that spring. But she and

Phil really have little in common. In order to keep him, she must maintain her artificial personality and pretend a consuming interest in his red auto, while his jealous possessiveness separates her from her friends. They quarrel, finally, the night before the annual Essay Contest, so that Betsy loses to Joe Willard for the second time running—yet breaking up with Phil leaves her newly at peace with herself. Trying to be what she isn't has given her a surer sense of what she is, and what really matters to her.

Betsy in Spite of Herself transports the reader to turn-of-the-century Minnesota, in part through an abundance of authentic detail. Unlike many historical novelists for the young, however, Maud Hart Lovelace selects details for their personal rather than their informative value. What gets mentioned is what matters to Betsy. For Betsy, 1907–08 is the year that the local hotel opens a Moorish Cafe with "hoochy-koochy music," the year that Julia makes a special trip to the Twin Cities to hear Geraldine Farrar and Enrico Caruso, the year that "The Merry Widow" waltz becomes the rage and she gets a Merry Widow hat for Easter. The perspective is limited—for Betsy at fifteen, in her small midwestern town, national politics and social problems do not exist—but vividly real within its boundaries. And this helps convince us that we are not merely reading about a girl of that period, but living her life.

Our desire to live that life helps to convince us too. For being Betsy is not simply being free from major problems; it is positive happiness—in large part, because she has the gift for happiness. She delights in the adventure of traveling on her own to Milwaukee in the parlor car, in dressing for her first dance, in a picnic with Tacy or a trip with Tib to the theater. Small things, too—the smell of books in the library, whipped cream on her coffee in Milwaukee, the first flowers in the spring, the first fires of fall. It makes sense that unlike her ambitious sister Julia, Betsy "had clung to every phase of childhood as it passed. She always wanted to keep life from going forward too fast" (*Betsy and Joe* 4).

The name Deep Valley suggests Betsy's attachment to her own childhood—a cozy, hidden place, a kind of womb—yet Betsy feels the attraction of the Great World as well. She and Tacy have always planned to travel abroad someday, and eventually Betsy will spend a wonderful year in Europe on her own. For all their emphasis on the happiness of home, a bright thread of internationalism—a positive experience of other lands and cultures—runs through the series. Betsy, Tacy and Tib become friendly with a colony of Syrian immigrants in *Over the Big Hill*. And Betsy's Christmas visit to Milwaukee— "'so German that it's like a foreign city,'" her father tells her (103)— foreshadows her stay in Munich in *Betsy and the Great World*.[2]

Betsy-Tacy was published in 1940; the series is basically a product of World War II and its aftermath, a period when many writers for children were hoping to sow the seeds of world citizenship. But Lovelace may have had another, more personal motive for stressing intercultural understanding. Her lifelong friend, Midge Gerlach—the real "Tib Muller"—was, like Tib, of German descent (Frisch 10). Lovelace may have suffered vicariously both for "Tib" and for the friends she had made in Germany, during the fiercely anti-German periods of both World Wars.

Her response was not to deny or tone down Tib's German heritage, but to emphasize it. Tib's slight accent and German phrases, her way with *Hasenpfeffer* and dumplings, became part of her special charm in the later books. In *Betsy in Spite of Herself*—published in 1946—Betsy thoroughly enjoys her introduction to Tib's ethnic milieu, which reminds her of her beloved Grimms' fairy tales, and picks up some German phrases for her "Dramatic and Mysterious" personality. In *Betsy and the Great World*, she spends several months in Munich, gaining a deeper appreciation of German culture, yet recoiling from the militarism and rigid class barriers Lovelace had observed on her own visit to Munich in 1914. A beautiful cup, touched by the lips of Goethe, and given to Betsy in Munich by a German friend, stands in a place of honor in her first married home—even though Germany and America are then on the brink of war.

Lovelace makes clear, too, that many German-Americans—the "Forty-eighters"—had originally left Germany to avoid its growing militarism, and did not support German policies in World War I. In Milwaukee, Betsy meets Tib's grandfather, the proud son of Forty-eighter revolutionaries. "'Here is no Kaiser,'" he tells her happily, "'no *Soldaten*

marching, marching all de time. Kaisers are *nicht gut'''* (149).
And in *Betsy's Wedding*, Tib promptly corrects Betsy's
assumption that she must sympathize with the German cause in
World War I. "'Of course I love the German people. But you
must remember that Grosspapa Hornik was a Forty-eighter,'"
she reminds her friend (98).

Such reminders of earlier episodes in the series are typical
of the technique with which Lovelace develops long-range
themes. As with the Little House books, the sheer length of this
series creates its own sense of reality; to a certain extent, the
reader inhabits the same time frame as the characters. And
maturation seems more plausible, when its development need
not be compressed into two hundred pages. In too many novels
for young people, some natural disaster or highly unlikely
catastrophe must be invoked to lend credibility to an overnight
conversion from childhood. Betsy's growth in independence and
responsibility can be as gradual, her moments of illumination as
infrequent as in real life. Throughout the series, references to
earlier books are a means of showing both Betsy and the reader
her step-by-step progress toward maturity.

At the beginning of *Heaven to Betsy*, Betsy spends a week
with a farm family, the Taggarts, and is miserably homesick. In
Betsy in Spite of Herself she worries whether she will be homesick
again in Milwaukee. "'Tib's different from the Taggarts
though,'" she tells herself, "'and I'm more than a year older'"
(l04). In *Betsy and Joe*, she spends a week with another farm
family and is reminded once more "how homesick she had been
at the Taggarts four years ago. . . . Now she was happy from
morning until night" (204–5). Such references create the illusion
of real experience, because they make use of the reader's long-
term memory as well as Betsy's.

Of course, what stands out in *Betsy in Spite of Herself* is not
Betsy's maturity, but the absurdity of her attempt to assume
what seems to her a more mature personality. But it's clear that
for Lovelace, such mistakes are a natural part of growing up. The
pattern is repeated in each of the high school books; Betsy
realizes that she has got off on a wrong tack once again—and
yet, volume by volume, the *nature* of her mistakes is changing.
The elementary uncertainty over her own identity in *Betsy in*

Spite of Herself has been succeeded in *Betsy and Joe* by uncertainty over how best to handle a complex relationship with two young men who love her. In three years she has progressed from a concern almost exclusively with herself to a sense of responsibility for those she cares for.

Like maturation, friendship is a very common theme in children's books; yet again, what Lovelace does with it is unusual. "Betsy and Tacy and Tib were three little girls who were friends," begins *Betsy-Tacy and Tib*. "They never quarreled." The joys of friendship dominate the early books; more surprisingly, they retain great importance all the way through *Betsy's Wedding*. It is one of the oldest antifeminist canards that true friendship between women is impossible, because they must constantly compete for male attention. Even in children's books, female characters often confine their long-term friendships to male friends or sisters. But far from abandoning her special relationship with Tacy and Tib when she grows interested in boys, Betsy expands her circle of friendship to include the Crowd. When her romance with Phil Brandish threatens her friendships, it is not Phil who wins.

In the early books, Lovelace wanted to show that three girls could be real friends and co-exist without quarreling; in the later books, she depicts female friendships capable of outlasting growth and change and puberty, even separation and marriage. Many of her characters, she writes in "About the Author," "are based on real people, still dear friends after many years." Perhaps she hoped to share with girl readers her knowledge that such friendships were possible, and worth trying for.

Internationalism, maturation, and friendship are themes that continue through the series, and whose effect is cumulative. More conspicuous in the high school quartet are the themes of individual integrity, and the relationship of the individual to her social group. Here is a real crux for Betsy. She is naturally a social creature; as even the hyphen in Betsy-Tacy intimates, she tends to define herself in terms of her friends and what they expect of her. The focal point of her high school years is the Crowd. As a freshman, in *Heaven to Betsy*, she all but abandons her writing, because it makes her feel out-of-step with her new friends:

> Writing didn't seem to fit in with the life she was living
> now. Carney didn't write; Bonnie didn't write. Betsy felt
> almost ashamed of her ambition. The boys teased her
> about being a Little Poetess. She felt that she would die if
> anyone discovered those poems in the handkerchief box,
> and the bits of stories she still wrote sometimes when she
> was supposed to be doing algebra. (144–5)

By the end of the book, however, Betsy realizes that
writing is essential to her. "What would life be like without her
writing? Writing filled her life with beauty and mystery, gave it
purpose . . . and promise" (258).

But this affirmation does not prevent her from making a
similar mistake in the aptly named *Betsy in Spite of Herself*. The
desire to claim a new, adult identity is natural enough. Many of
us will remember assuming a new first name at around this age,
or at least a new way of spelling it. Young readers will enjoy the
imaginative thoroughness with which Betsy carries out her
scheme—plotting her own life like a true novelist. They will also
see where she goes wrong, both in devaluing what she is and in
pretending to be what she isn't. They may smile at Betsy's "List
of Things I Must Do to be Different," which begins

1. Start signing your name Betsye.

2. Don't laugh so much.

3. Seldom smile.

4. Keep your voice low.

5. Wear green. (174)

And they may notice that it is not really about *being* but about
seeming different—about creating an image rather than a reality.

They may even recognize Betsy's false image of herself as
stereotypically feminine. When Phil, for example, begins talking
about his auto on their first date, Betsy pretends to be fascinated:

> He talked on, comparing Steamers and Buicks in technical
> detail. No one could have comprehended less of this than
> Betsy but at least she knew well that when a man talks it is
> a woman's part to listen. She listened, starry-eyed.
>
> "The Buick must be ever so much better!"
>
> He tightened his grasp on her arm.

"In the spring, maybe we'll go for a whirl." (198–9)

Later, when Carney invites her to join a new Girls Debating Club, Betsy refuses; she "thought debating sounded intellectual, unfeminine. She thought Phil wouldn't like it. She said no" (216). One of her first acts after breaking up with Phil is to volunteer for the Debating Club. By the time she travels to Europe, alone, Betsy will be calling herself a suffragette (*Great World* 70), and the man she will marry has always thought of her as a fellow writer and a professional.

Throughout the high school stories, Joe Willard stands for Betsy as something more than an attractive male.[3] She speaks to him in English class on the first day of her sophomore year:

"Read *Ivanhoe*?" she asked hastily.

"Of course. Why?" He sounded puzzled.

"Don't you remember? Gaston told us to read it over the summer. None of the kids have read it. They're having fits."

"You've read it, haven't you?"

"Yes. But I'm not admitting it."

He looked at her keenly.

"You wouldn't!" he said.

Now what did he mean by that? Betsy wondered, blushing again. Did he know she was so dissatisfied with herself that she was always pretending to be different? Probably he did, and despised her for it. More than any one she knew, Joe Willard was always, fearlessly, himself. (30)

Betsy admires the proud integrity she dare not imitate. The persistence of Betsy's interest in Joe through her four years of high school is like a promise that she too will someday be able to stand on her own. Later that same fall, she passes a kind of test. Her English teacher, Mr. Gaston, criticizes her in class for using the word "rosy" in a story to describe apple blossoms. "Apple blossoms, my dear young lady, aren't pink. They are white" (84). Mortified but stubborn, Betsy refuses to call pink blossoms white—and Joe, to everyone's astonishment, supports her. For the first time, she has defended her integrity as a writer, and the small incident creates a new bond between them.

But I've said that these books are more complex than they seem, and *Betsy in Spite of Herself* is no simple battlefield where truth and the individual win out over falsehood and conformity. To Betsy's surprise, Julia suggests that "'the whole affair did you a lot of good'"—and not just by teaching her to be herself:

> "You're better groomed, more poised, you have sweeter manners and . . . well . . . more charm than you had before you started it. Don't be scornful of 'la de da,' Bettina. You may want to use it sometime with someone you really like."
>
> "But then," cried Betsy, "surely I wouldn't have to use it! Not with someone who was my own kind!"
>
> "Oh . . . wouldn't you?" asked Julia. (264)

Just when Betsy—and the reader—is sure she has decoded the value system, Julia claims a place in it for artifice as well as honesty.

At the same time, Betsy is discovering an unsuspected vulnerability in Joe. At one point he haughtily rebuffs her suggestion that he join her Crowd, insisting that it would bore him (72–3). She is hurt and angry. But after that conversation with Julia, she seeks out Joe's friend, the town librarian Miss Sparrow; she learns that he is an orphan and entirely self-supporting, with no time or money for "'the boy and girl pleasures.'" "'He wouldn't like coming to call on you in shabby clothes,'" Miss Sparrow explains. "'When you urge him to come he gets desperate'" (269). Betsy realizes that Julia is right; she will need tact and charm as well as honesty to deal with this proud boy. "Next year, she resolved, she would find some way to make a friend of Joe . . . and without making things hard for him either" (269). Later, in *Betsy and Joe*, she will learn that not even falling in love can solve all their problems—later still, that she needs all her intelligence to create a happy marriage.

In *Betsy in Spite of Herself* Betsy discovers that she wants other things more than the feminine power-symbol of a rich and handsome male. She wants her writing more—it is despite Phil's disapproval that she enters the Essay Contest—and all that her writing means to her in terms of her true self. She wants her real friends more, and the simple pleasures that she so much enjoys. "'I wanted the picnic more, and not hurting Tom's feelings. I wanted . . . my freedom more'" (264). But she also discovers that simply knowing what she wants isn't enough; dealing with real people requires charm and tact—even calculation.

Betsy may wear pink ribbons on her corset cover, and if she were alive she would be a centenarian, but her mistakes, her problems, her joy in living and in exploring other cultures, and her wide-eyed discoveries still make good reading—not only for the women who were girls yesterday, but for the women who are girls today.

NOTES

1. In addition to the Betsy-Tacy stories, Lovelace wrote three other books with Deep Valley characters, in which Betsy plays a minor role: *Winona's Pony Cart* (1953) for younger children, and *Carney's House Party* (1949) and *Emily of Deep Valley* (1950) for teenagers. Both Carney and Emily, especially, are proof that Lovelace could successfully conceive a heroine very different from Betsy (or herself).

2. For Betsy, Milwaukee has always epitomized foreignness. As far back as *Betsy-Tacy*, an imaginary trip to Milwaukee with Tacy becomes an exotic adventure:

> "See those towers a way, way off?" Betsy said. And
> when they had come closer, she said, "It looks like the
> cities on my Sunday School cards, with that wall and
> all those towers."
> "That's right," said Tacy. "I see palm trees." (88–9)

3. Lovelace's development of Joe Willard's special role was one of her greatest departures from autobiography. Although Joe is based on her husband Delos, the two did not meet until after Lovelace had graduated from high school (Frisch 20).

WORKS CITED

The Betsy-Tacy Society Newsletter. Mankato, Minn.: Betsy-Tacy Society, 1990– .

Frisch, Carlienne A. *Betsy-Tacy in Deep Valley: People and Places*. Mankato, Minn.: Friends of the Minnesota Valley Regional Library, 1987.

Lovelace, Maud Hart. "About the Author." Dust jacket of *Betsy and Tacy Go Downtown*. New York: Crowell, 1943.

———. *Betsy and Joe*. New York: Crowell, 1948.

———. *Betsy and the Great World*. New York: Crowell, 1952.

———. *Betsy in Spite of Herself*. New York: Crowell, 1946.

———. *Betsy's Wedding*. New York: Crowell, 1955.

———. *Betsy-Tacy*. New York: Crowell, 1940.

———. *Betsy-Tacy and Tib*. New York: Crowell, 1941.

———. *Heaven to Betsy*. New York: Crowell, 1945.

Cat-Child: Two Cat Stories by Beverly Cleary and Ursula Moray Williams

"I had rather be a kitten, and cry mew."

(Henry IV, Part I)

More cats than dogs play the lead role in children's books. In most dog stories the dog-owner, not the dog, provides the primary point of view. Typically, as in Jim Kjelgaard's *Big Red* or Mary Stolz's *A Dog on Barkham Street*, the plot hinges on a boy's desire for a dog or his problems with it; most of the better-known exceptions—*Lad, Lassie-Come-Home, White Fang, The Call of the Wild*—were written for adults. In cat stories the cat sits at the center, and the reader sees through the cat-eyes of Jenny Linsky, Tom Kitten, Buttons, and Orlando. Cats often dominate even a human protagonist; they run the show in *The Cat in the Hat* and *Time Cat*, and in *Millions of Cats* overwhelm us by sheer numbers.

The comparative rarity of dog protagonists can be accounted for by the common view of dogs as wholly dependent on human beings for their fulfillment. The classic boy-wants-dog story is a kind of proto-love story, in which the dog's unquestioning devotion is highly satisfying to the (usually male) protagonist. Most children naturally prefer to identify with the power position in this relationship; all but helpless in a world dominated by adults who may or may not care for them, they find consolation in the dog's faithful and dependent love. Sometimes authors create humor by reversing the dog-human roles—in Alexandra Day's "Carl" series and Dodie Smith's *The*

101 Dalmations, wise dogs take care of their human friends—but the humans remain objects of doggy love.

The cat-human relationship is far more ambiguous, and as a result, cats play more varied roles in children's literature. A cat may be a magical guide, an urbane adult, a toughminded nonconformist—and often, the child itself.

The common view of cats as essentially independent of human society, as well as the tradition linking cats with witches and sorcerers, is reflected in the cat's literary role as magical guide or intermediary. In cat stories of this type, the cat dominates the young protagonist—whether providing for his welfare as an animal helper (as in "Puss in Boots"), initiating him into another world (as in Lloyd Alexander's *Time Cat* or Nicholas Stuart Gray's *Grimbold's Other World*), or inciting magical anarchy in this one (as in Dr. Seuss's *The Cat in the Hat*).

Other cat stories, in which human beings are often of peripheral importance, imagine a feline society parallel to ours. The British folktale "The King of the Cats" suggests that the cat drowsing by the fireside may have a secret, even royal identity in its own world. The "Cat Club" series of Esther Averill and Kathleen Hale's "Orlando" books portray cat societies in tireless and loving detail. In *Old Possum's Book of Practical Cats* by T.S. Eliot, cats simply enter human society on equal terms. Stories such as these allow children to identify with protagonists who are in charge of their own lives, like adults, yet who also suggest alternatives to adult supremacy.

In still other stories the cat's role is that of the nonconforming individual. Disobedient Tom Kitten climbs up a chimney and into terrible trouble in *The Roly-Poly Pudding*. Ernest Thompson-Seton's "Slum Cat" stubbornly prefers her lower-class milieu, and escapes from a life of pampered luxury to find her way back to the slums. Rudyard Kipling, a cat-person who wanted to be a dog-person, seems to have expressed his ambivalence about his own nonconformity in "The Cat Who Walked by Himself." Although at the end of the story the cat succeeds in setting his own terms with society, he must pay the price of perpetual hostility from leaders (the Man) and followers (the Dog) alike. Lewis Carroll's Cheshire Cat, which cheerfully admits to its own madness, is another nonconformist—the only

Rudyard Kipling's own striking illustration for "The Cat Who Walked by Himself" from *Just So Stories* emphasizes the utter solitude of the cat "walking by his wild lone through the Wet Wild Woods and waving his wild tail." *Just So Stories* (Garden City, N.Y.: Doubleday, 1902).

inhabitant of Wonderland who treats Alice with courtesy or whom Alice herself considers a "friend." William Empson suggests in *Some Versions of Pastoral* that the Cat and Alice are in fact "the same sort of thing," and represent Carroll's own "ideal of intellectual detachment." The Cat, he says,

> can disappear because it can abstract itself into a more interesting inner world; it appears only as a head because it is almost a disembodied intelligence, and only as a grin because it can impose an atmosphere without being present. In frightening the king by the allowable act of looking at him it displays the soul-force of Mr. Gandhi; it is unbeheadable because its soul cannot be killed. . . . (273)

Unlike Kipling, Carroll presents his nonconforming cat as serenely invulnerable even to the highest social authorities, the King and Queen.

In addition to social and intellectual nonconformists, we find the creative nonconformist—the artist—symbolized by a blue cat in Catherine Cate Coblentz's *The Blue Cat of Castle Town*. The blue cat listens to the river singing, "'Riches will pass and power. Beauty remains./ Sing your own song'" (16), and sets out to find a home with someone who will sing the song of beauty with him. After several mistaken choices, the cat settles down with a bitter, unattractive, but talented young woman who weaves its portrait into her carpet—a real carpet, by the way, which now hangs in the Metropolitan Museum as a masterpiece of American folk art. In this tale the typical independence of the stray cat, which chooses its own home, is equated with the artist's need to protect creative integrity by refusing to live with the shoddy or commercially successful.[1]

But most often the stray cat is clearly a child in search of the love and security of a family. Tom Robinson's picture book *Buttons*, about a tough alley tom who must overcome his distrust of all humanity, is a good realistic story of this kind. Wanda Gag's *Millions of Cats* takes the viewpoint of the adopting family, which has to choose one cat out of the "millions and billions and trillions of cats" eager for a home. Paul Gallico's *The Silent Miaow*, though written for adults, is also an adoption story, in the form of advice to strays on how to choose and ingratiate oneself into a suitable household. The happy endings of such cat-orphan stories must be reassuring (or, if need be, comforting) to young readers, for whom loss of home and family is the ultimate imaginable disaster.

And yet, some cat stories are not so reassuring—those stories in which the feline protagonist seeks love and security, but finds rejection. As a motif, it is even traditional; all "Puss in Boots" variants begin with the disappointment of the youngest son who has received "only a cat" as his inheritance, and are motivated by the cat's need to prove its usefulness. In Perrault's version, the miller's son is about to kill and skin his legacy, who hastily offers a more profitable suggestion. Nor is "Dick Whittington," from the cat's point of view, an edifying legend; Dick is only too willing to turn his faithful pet into an investment. Elizabeth Coatsworth's *The Cat Who Went to Heaven* also employs this motif, adding a religious dimension; the little cat Good Fortune must prove herself worthy not only of a place in the artist's household but of one by Buddha's side as well. Despite her sweet temper and virtuous behavior, the artist repeatedly insults and rejects her, and even the happy ending is qualified by her death.

The title of Paul Gallico's *The Abandoned* (written for adults but often read by children) signals the centrality of its rejection motif. Its protagonist is a small boy named Peter, transformed after a near-fatal accident into a white cat. Even as a boy, Peter had been emotionally abandoned by his mother, who "never seemed to have much time for him" (5). Now his nanny, failing to recognize him in his new form, drives him out into the terrifying city streets. Jennie, the cat who befriends him, has also been abandoned by her human "family"; she has sworn that she will "'never again trust a human being, or give them love or live with them'" (61). Indeed, the entire story is revealed, in the end, to have been Peter's own delirious fantasy, and the happy ending is his repentant mother's promise that "'There is nothing I will not try to do to make you happy if you will just get strong and well once more'" (303).

Such stories as these spring from the cat's unique position in human society—now valued, now vilified, with an ambivalence directed toward no other domestic animal. On the child's level, however, their import is human and universal. No child escapes the hurtful experience of rejection. Thus, the cat protagonist becomes cat-child; its sufferings express the child's worst fears of being unloved, abandoned, cast out into a hostile world.

Two children's books seem to me worth examining in detail for their particularly insightful treatments of this theme: *Socks* (1973) by Beverly Cleary and *Island Mackenzie* (1960) by Ursula Moray Williams.[2] In both, the cat-child protagonist provides a way of exploring painful and complex psychological aspects of family life that might otherwise be judged unsuitable for a young audience.

Socks the cat is adopted by a young couple, the Brickers, and becomes "the center of the Bricker household" (36), till a baby arrives. Then he is ignored, unpetted, underfed (in his opinion), and finally (after biting Mrs. Bricker's ankle) forced to live outdoors, where a mean tomcat bullies him and steals his food. After he is beaten up by the tomcat, the Brickers allow him indoors again, but the attention and affection he had once taken for granted are his no longer. The solution lies in a new alliance between Socks and the fast-growing baby, Charles William. Alone for the first time one afternoon, they discover each other as playmates, make a thorough mess of the bedroom, and curl up to sleep together, friends for keeps.

Socks is truly both cat and child, and his story can be taken literally; it is not uncommon for a cat or dog in a previously childless household to cause difficulties when a new baby comes. His behavior is authentic in every pungent detail, and cat-owners may argue that his motivations and thought processes are too. When shut into the laundry room for the night, for example,

> Socks lay yowling on the hard floor and groped under the door with his paw. He sat up and threw his shoulder against the door. When nothing, absolutely nothing would free him, his last act before settling down on the sweat shirt was to plow Kitty Litter over the floor so someone would have to sweep it up in the morning. (105–6)

But his feelings are human and described in human terms—the feelings of a child displaced by a new brother or sister:

Sad and confused, Socks went back to lapping up the formula in the bowl. The warmth and sweetness of the milk comforted him. He lapped every drop and then licked the empty dish so hard that he moved it across the newspaper until it bumped the wall. Socks needed every drop of consolation he could get. His owners loved the baby more than they loved him. (54)

Moving an empty food dish by licking it is something that cats really do. But words like "sad and confused," "comforted," and "loved" encourage the young reader to empathize with Socks as though he were a fellow child. At the same time, Beverly Cleary maintains a careful distance between child reader and cat character, by making Socks's behavior so wholly catlike, and by her pervasive, ironic humor. For a young reader, this balance between distance and involvement is especially delicate; while an adult reader can take the story lightly and may perceive it as pure comedy, a young reader may find Socks's problems almost too true to be funny. A number of my students had read *Socks* as children. When I asked them if they remembered it as "sad" or "funny," they looked doubtful. They remembered that they "felt sorry" for Socks—but also that there was "a happy ending."

This balance between emotional involvement and ironic detachment is characteristic of Beverly Cleary, and makes all her books read differently for adults and children, even for older and younger children. There is a scene in *Ramona and Her Father*, for example, in which Ramona's father comes home so late that Ramona, waiting alone outside the empty house, begins to think he may have gone for good. An adult reader knows that Ramona is being melodramatic and finds the scene amusing; a child reader will not be so sure. For both, however, the scene is given a moving undertone, as Ramona realizes for the first time how deeply she needs her father.

Equally characteristic of Cleary is the complexity of her point of view, her insistence that children and adults make an effort to understand each other. In *Socks* we are always aware of Socks's feelings, but we do not see the Brickers through his eyes alone. We hear Mrs. Bricker's "small, scared voice"(38) as she realizes that her labor has begun, and the anxious discussion over the first home feeding and burping of Charles William. "Both parents spoke of the baby as 'he,'" observes the author wryly, "as if he were a stranger whose name they had not caught" (45). When the Brickers banish Socks from the house—a crucial scene—the viewpoint shuttles rapidly between them and him. The young reader, however unused to empathizing with harried mothers, is forced to see how "A fussy, teething baby, a husband in a hurry to leave for his classes and his job in the University library, the strain of a mother-in-law in a house too small for guests, papers waiting to be typed, and a nipping cat were all too much for Mrs. Bricker" (117).

Even Charles William acquires his own perspective, as soon as he begins to discover the world around him:

> Charles William stared at his toe in astonishment. Never before had he experienced Scotch tape on his toe. He lay back and waved his foot. The tape stuck fast. Fascinating! "Ah-gah-gah," he said. (90)

Awareness of these several points of view makes the final reconciliation of all parties in a new family configuration particularly satisfying. But it also encourages young readers to move beyond natural egocentricity toward a mature regard for the rights and feelings of other people—even to recognize their own self-regard for what it is. Socks, with whom the reader must identify, is not simply a victim of injustice and insensitivity; he is spoiled, greedy, inconsiderate, and thoroughly self-centered. And Beverly Cleary is too cunning to call him any of these things. She tells us that Socks is "affectionate toward his loving owners but firm about getting his own way" (36), or that Socks liked to distract Mrs. Bricker from her typing because "Her typewriter was his rival for her attention, and Socks did not like rivals" (35). By using language that Socks himself might choose, she allows us to see through it and make our own judgment on his behavior.

But Beverly Cleary's refusal to label Socks "spoiled" and "selfish" is more than a technique for disarming and educating the young reader. It is also a way of acknowledging the real suffering of the displaced child. She knows that what the child is afraid of losing is not pampering, but love: "He was filled with jealousy and anger and a terrible anxiety. The Brickers might love the new pet more than they loved him" (43). And again, a few pages later, "His owners loved the baby more than they loved him" (54). When Socks has just been cast out of the house, we hear Charles William shouting "Oy-doy-doy!"—"happy to be eating breakfast at last and secure in the love of his family" (119).

Again, readers of different ages may be differently affected. Adults may be reminded of the need for love that underlies the child's most obnoxious behavior. Children may be reassured by the open acceptance and kind understanding of their most painful feelings—and especially when the story reaches them through a parent's voice, read aloud and shared.

Beverly Cleary offers sympathy, but no easy way out. From the hour of Charles William's arrival, it is clear that Socks will never again be "the center of the Bricker household." The Brickers will always love Charles William more than they love him. He must content himself with whatever love they have left over, and by learning to care for the child who has displaced him. The solution is neither wishful nor sentimental, but almost grimly realistic.

In *Socks* the cat-child identification is obvious; the setting is here and now, and the situation a common family problem. The same cannot be said of *Island Mackenzie*, a more complex and fantastic variation on the theme. Its marvelous opening sentence propels the reader into a dramatic and exotic world:

> One August afternoon a little shipwrecked cat called Mackenzie was swimming for his life toward a desert island, pursued by eight hungry sharks.
>
> Far behind him the remains of a typhoon still harassed the southern horizon. Beyond that a rescue ship, summoned by wireless, hurried to pick up survivors from the wreck of the pleasure steamer *Marigold*, but the cat knew nothing of this and swam far beyond their aid. His natural intelligence told him that land was not far away, while his stout heart and strongly thrashing claws served to keep him just beyond the range of the terrible danger on his tail. (11–12)

Mackenzie's ship, the *Marigold*, has been sunk by the typhoon, separating him from his beloved master, Captain Jupiter Foster. Having reached the island just ahead of the sharks, Mackenzie finds another surviving passenger, Miss Mary Pettifer, and attempts to make friends with her. Unfortunately, Miss Pettifer hates cats, and the fact that she happens to be in love with Captain Foster only makes her jealous of Mackenzie. She drives him away with well-aimed coconuts, and when he accidentally unravels her knitting—a striped sweater she has been making for Captain Foster—she decides to kill him. Ruthlessly trapping him in her knitting bag, she plunges it into a tide pool. She repents in time to fish him out alive, however, and they eventually become truly devoted to each other. They save each other from an enormous python, and from cannibals, and survive a fire that burns the island bare. And when Captain Foster, seeing the smoke, arrives in his new ship to rescue them, all three are ready to settle down together and live happily ever after.

Like *Socks*, *Island Mackenzie* is best read aloud to children too young to tackle it on their own—children just beyond the picture book stage and ready for a "chapter" book. Really good stories for these five-to-eight-year-olds are rare, and few are as thrilling as *Island Mackenzie*. Socks, a more typical protagonist for this age group, is at worst beaten up—quite vividly—by the tomcat. Mackenzie is nearly devoured by sharks, nearly drowned by Miss Pettifer, actually swallowed and all but digested by the python, captured after a fierce battle by the cannibals, and half boiled alive in their pot. And the style is designed to match. Borrowing the ornate language of Victorian popular fiction, it achieves a kind of heroic elevation—"his stout heart and strongly thrashing claws"—that descends abruptly to the mock-heroic when the "claws" remind us that our valiant hero is a cat. Sentences are far longer and more intricately structured than is usual in young children's books, and the vocabulary larger and more interesting, full of words like "impervious," "gratification," and "promontory." The author, moreover, has an expert's knowledge of what young listeners can comprehend, and deftly varies her mixture with short sentences and punchy verbs, while hair-raising adventures alternate with pleasant details of life on the island—Mackenzie's fishing and Miss Pettifer's gardening.

Finally, for all the violent action and cliffhanging suspense, the changing relationship of Miss Pettifer and Mackenzie is what remains most important. Its solid and complex emotional core makes *Island Mackenzie* much more than a funny adventure story. A crucial difference between *Socks* and *Island Mackenzie* is the developmental stage of the protagonist. Socks's emotions and thought processes are those of a young child—or even, plausibly, a real cat. Mackenzie's, though characterized by a childlike simplicity, are closer to those of a boy in his teens, or even a young man with a strong sense of responsibility. Unlike Socks, who expects to be looked after by the Brickers, Mackenzie feels duty-bound to protect Miss Pettifer. He resolves to guard her while she sleeps, even after she has thrown coconuts at him:

> "For this human being is not kind," said Mackenzie to himself, "but she is one of the passengers from the *Marigold*. I must see that no harm comes to her, even if I don't sleep a wink myself till morning." (46)

Next morning he provides fish for her to eat; after they have become friends, he even risks death to save her from the python and the cannibals.

In fact, though he first crawls into her lap (while she sleeps) for comfort, like a child, his relationship with Miss Pettifer at once becomes that of a man romantically—even sexually—in love. When his initial advances are rudely repulsed, and she throws him from her lap and hurls coconuts at him, he is "miserably humiliated" (43) and thinks "What a way for a lady to behave!" (44). Yet he cannot stop following and watching her from a distance. He feels respect for her courage on the crocodile-infested beach, and for her ability to swim and throw (89). (Miss Pettifer is no standardized old maid.) His impulse to "play and show off a little" (54), when she first allows him to approach her, shows his desire to impress her. Overexcited by his success, however, he makes a predatory leap, which not only unravels the sweater but plunges his claws into the lady's thigh (58). Again, he has gone too far, and again she recoils with anger. In her vengeful attempt to murder him, however, she learns that she does care for him after all, and after she has rubbed him back to life with her skirt, they sleep "side by side by the light of the great tropical moon" (67).

Significantly, a few nights later Mackenzie dreams vividly of mermaids who try to lure him into the sea. Miss Pettifer rescues him from them and then slaps him soundly, exclaiming, "'Can't a man ever tell a hussy when he sees one?'" (73). "But the mermaids," Mackenzie remembers afterwards, "had been very beautiful and charming," and he lies half awake, "thinking about them for some while . . ." (75).

The love growing between Miss Pettifer and Mackenzie is not sweet and simple; it is an intense and often difficult relationship. Mackenzie is still tempted by "other women" in his dreams. And Miss Pettifer is unfaithful to him in another fashion. She finds a baby parrot with a broken wing, nurses it back to health, and becomes for a time totally absorbed in the "ugly little creature" (85). Mackenzie is extremely jealous, and it is not until he nearly dies in the python's belly, and she rescues him, that they are reconciled once more.

The developing relationship thus roughly parallels a human courtship and marriage—but only roughly. While Mackenzie's jealousy can be compared to the feelings of some young fathers, the parrot is in no sense "his," or really even Miss Pettifer's, and can be disposed of guiltlessly in the next thunderstorm. Recovered from her infatuation, Miss Pettifer does not even "turn a hair at finding the parrot lying dead on the edge of the jungle" (98). And the final *ménage a trois* of Mackenzie, Miss Pettifer, and Captain Foster has no imaginable adult human equivalent. Both these "solutions" suggest a level at which *Island Mackenzie* regresses from adult romance to wish-fulfilling Oedipal fantasy: the child (Mackenzie), finding the mother (Miss Pettifer) temporarily separated from the father (Captain Foster), eventually overcomes her irrational hostility and wins her love; vanquishes its one rival, a younger sibling (the parrot); and finally re-forms the family unit with itself at the center, as Captain Foster, "Taking her in his arms, with only Mackenzie to separate the beating of their two hearts," asks Miss Pettifer to marry him and she replies, "'Love me, love my cat!'" (126). Her use of animal characters allows the author—and reader—to make the book work both ways.

If *Socks* holds a mirror to the young reader, *Mackenzie* lets children see themselves as older and more heroic than they are.

It says less of their common problems than of love-relationships that still lie ahead—yet in ways that children can relate to the loves they know.

Both tales, despite their humor, make painful reading. Socks and Mackenzie suffer rejection, indignity, and neglect from those they care for. Both come to know the "dark side" of love—for those we love are also those who make us suffer most.

Indeed, these cat tales depict aspects of human family life that one might hesitate to include in a "realistic" story. In Beverly Cleary's "Ramona" books, Beezus is sometimes resentful of her little sister and feels that their parents favor Ramona over her. Beezus is wrong, of course. But in *Socks* the older "child" is right; the Brickers do care more for Charles William than they do for him. We see this clearly, and we share his jealousy and distress. The animal fantasy actually brings into prominence negative aspects of parenting and family relationships that are played down by the "realistic" family story, but are nonetheless often "real," whether literally or simply as experienced by a child.

Island Mackenzie moves further down the scale of horrors, from mere neglect to open hostility, physical abuse, and attempted murder. If *Socks* exposes the unhappiness that is possible even in happy families, the jungle island uncovers the dark and primitive passions lurking even in the most ladylike; crocodiles, pythons, and cannibals prove less savage than the mother-lover with her knitting bag. The grimmest "problem novels" generally stop short of this. Yet the cat-mask enables the young reader to contemplate these frightening aspects of human nature with equanimity—as an animal's "flight distance" is decreased by the interposition of a pane of glass.

These cat stories, of course, do not stand alone. A hundred and fifty years ago, Hans Christian Andersen used an ugly duckling to represent both the artist-nonconformist and the abandoned child. Animal protagonists have been employed by many authors to reveal the human dark side as it affects both animal and human victims. Stories of hunting and other animal-slaying sports, like *Bambi* and *Ferdinand*, may call into question the human need to kill not only animals but one's own kind. Horse stories like *Black Beauty* and *King of the Wind* show how cruelly society treats all helpless creatures. But stories of the cat-child, centered on the most intimate relationships—those within the family—are closest to home. What happens to Socks and Mackenzie can happen to anyone.

Both cats begin—as we all do—by taking love for granted. Both learn how hurtful love can be. And both must prove themselves worthy of love by long, humiliating, even dangerous ordeals. And yet, after all, both stories end well. Love may never again offer that first careless security—but a wise cat can live happily with the family that is still its own.

NOTES

1. The carpet, known as the "Blue Cat Rug," was created by Zeruah Higley Guernsey of Castleton, Vermont, in 1835. Eighty squares of dark, homespun wool were elaborately embroidered with plants and animals, then stitched together.

Another author who saw cats and artists as connected was Margaret Wise Brown. For a discussion of her use of cats to represent her own creative process, see my "Cat-Quest: A Symbolic Animal in Margaret Wise Brown."

2. *Island Mackenzie* was first published in Great Britain in 1959 as *The Nine Lives of Island Mackenzie*. All references here are to the U.S. edition.

WORKS CITED

Cleary, Beverly. *Socks*. New York: William Morrow, 1973.

Coblentz, Catherine Cate. *The Blue Cat of Castle Town*. New York: Longmans, 1949.

Empson, William. *Some Versions of Pastoral*. London: Chatto and Windus, 1950.

Gallico, Paul. *The Abandoned*. New York: Knopf, 1950.

Rahn, Suzanne. "Cat-Quest: A Symbolic Animal in Margaret Wise Brown." *Children's Literature* 22 (1994): 149–161

Williams, Ursula Moray. *Island Mackenzie*. New York: William Morrow, 1960.

Beneath the Surface with *Fungus the Bogeyman*

It has been called "the nastiest book ever published for children" (Chambers 100), and it holds a pivotal position among the picture books of British artist Raymond Briggs. *Fungus the Bogeyman*, published in 1977 (first American edition 1979), offers the most fully developed fantasy and the most outrageous affront to adult mores of all Briggs's children's books. It also marks the philosophical midpoint of the twelve-year curve Raymond Briggs traced, book by book, from the cheerful confidence of *Jim and the Beanstalk* (1970) through the good-humored grumbling of *Father Christmas* (1973) and the melancholy of *The Snowman* (1978) to the black despair of *When the Wind Blows* (1982). *Fungus* reveals common concerns that unite the two extremes, and make the last book a wholly logical development from the first.

Bogies, according to K.M. Briggs's *Encyclopedia of Fairies*, comprise "a whole class of mischievous, frightening and even dangerous spirits whose delight it is to torment mankind" (30). From this basis in folklore, Briggs has extrapolated a race of large, blobby, green-skinned beings who inhabit their own world underground. At night (their day), the Bogeymen emerge to carry on their "work"—frightening human beings with mysterious footsteps, scrapings on windowpanes, and an occasional graveyard appearance; they also cause boils. But Briggs shows us the daily life of Fungus at home as well, eating breakfast with his wife and son, bicycling off to work, and stopping off at a pub on the way back. Meanwhile, an anonymous narrator fills in the picture of Bogeydom, lecturing in academic style on Bogey culture, sports, flora, fauna, and anatomy.

Both in form and in content, *Fungus the Bogeyman* could scarcely be better calculated to repel the adult reader—or intrigue the young one. In form it is what is sometimes called a "strip-format" book, a hardcover book designed like a comic strip to tell a story by means of a sequence of pictures, with multiple pictures to a page, dialogue in "balloons," and explanatory captions above or below the frame.[1] Such books have been popular in Europe for decades; Hergé's Tintin books have been admired even by adults for their graphic excellence, and *Asterix the Gaul* for its humor. They are at least tolerated on the margins of children's literature. In America, however, the strip-format never achieved hardcover status, and adult disapproval of softcover comics has been taken for granted since at least the 1940s.[2] Like several of Briggs's picture books, *Fungus* defies this long-standing prejudice. At first glance, it might even be mistaken for a rather large comic book, with frames, captions, and speech balloons; then we begin to notice how radically Briggs has modified the traditional format.

The color scheme is dominated not by primary colors but by soft shades of grass-green, blue-green, and brown in the background, setting off the brighter yellow-green of the Bogeymen. Moreover, a large proportion of each page is devoted to hand-lettered captions of extraordinary length that compete with or even overwhelm the pictures. There are actually more words per page than in many children's books of conventional design.

The truth of the matter is that *Fungus* requires and stimulates above-average literacy in its young readers. Its general reading level is at least sixth grade. In addition, scattered lavishly through its pages, are puns and other varieties of word play, literary allusions, quotations and misquotations (from authors like Milton, Keats, Shelley, and Tennyson), and obscure words like "scran," "dwine," and "hodmandod." Fungus himself and his family are avid readers. We are shown the shelves of a Bogey public library, and tacitly challenged to recognize the originals of such "adapted" titles as *Far from the Madding Bogey, A Portrait of the Artist as a Young Bogeyman, A Room with a Bogey,* and *A la Recherche de Bogeys Perdus* (28–9). *Fungus*, concludes Aidan Chambers (its most eloquent defender), "pretends to be anti-book and is actually formatively, lovingly book-bound" (102).

Indeed, for Chambers, *Fungus* is not subliterature (like the comic book), but advanced literature—a work that gives children a chance to meet "the ideas of post-Joycean fiction" on their own ground (102). Like the post-Joycean novel, *Fungus* displays

> An interest in the mosaic texture of life expressed in various modes (story, handbook-like explanations, diagrams, documentary reportage, overlays of feeling and perception, running gags, gossip, interior monologue— and on and on), rather than in a sequentially-told unwaveringly modulated narrative. . . . (103)

It plays games with the reader, calling attention to "the book as Book—as Object—and Fiction as Artifice" (103). At one point Briggs refers to "great literary works, such as this book you are reading" (29); at another, he covers the illustration of a Bogey lavatory with a black square labeled,

> The Publishers wish to state that this picture has been deleted in the interests of good taste and public decency.

As the Bogeymen set off to work on their bicycles, the caption at the bottom of the page reads, "They are on the way to THE SURFACE . . . To where WE live . . . TO WHERE YOU LIVE!" (9). And a great green hand rears out of the bottom margin pointing straight at you.

This element of play may be what makes the more esoteric literary devices and allusions intriguing rather than simply incomprehensible to young readers. On every page, they are challenged to observe and figure out all kinds of verbal and visual details, and rewarded with a joke when they succeed. If the adult titles in the Bogey library are beyond their reach, they can try their wits on the bookshelf of Fungus's son Mould, laden with such classic favorites as *Anne of Green Bogeys, Tom's Midnight Bogey, A Child's Garden of Bogeys*, and *The Tale of the Flopsy Bogies* (35).

Thus *Fungus* is first of all a joke on adults, with their bias against the "antiliterary" format of the comic strip—but also on children who expect an easy read. Its content is equally subversive, arousing prejudices far more deeply rooted than those against comic books, and with equally unexpected results.

Take, for example, the opening scene. It is sunset, the dawn of the Bogey day. Fungus and his wife Mildew are just awakening in their Bogeybed:

> Fungus: Oooh! What a night that was! This bed has almost dried up!
>
> Mildew: I know, drear. It needs more slime.
>
> Fungus: What a horrible day! Feels quite warm!
>
> Mildew: I hate this time of year. It's so light.
>
> Fungus [retrieving his clothes from a trough of water]: Ah! Nice wet dressing-gown and sabots!
>
> Mildew: I'll change the sheets today, drear. The dirt has almost worn off these.
>
> Fungus: I know, love, the smell's all gone. (3)

Even more disconcerting is the Bogey bathroom, where Fungus plasters his armpits with muck ("just add slime"), and the sink counter contains bottles of Eau de Colon, Femstench Rollon Odorant for Bogey Ladies, Faboge Pus, and Toilet Water (4). By this point, the adult reader may already have recoiled in disgust—even before watching the Bogey family at the breakfast table ("'These flaked corns are still a bit crisp, Mum—not mouldy at all'" [6]), or Fungus getting dressed ("The waterproof layer is not intended to keep the rain out, but rather to keep the Bogeyman's own natural secretions in" [5]). In our shower-a-day society, *Fungus* violates taboos as deeply entrenched as those related to sex, death, and religion—the taboos against dirtiness, against smelliness, against all those "natural secretions" that Bogeymen prize so highly.

There is no doubt that children find these taboos particularly titillating. Their idea of an obscene song is one that begins, "Great big gobs of greasy grimy gopher guts!" Is Raymond Briggs simply pandering to this youthful fascination with innards and excretia?

Some aspects of Bogeydom seem to fit this explanation; others do not. Bogeys do indeed relish damp, dirt, slime, and smelliness—their name for human beings is "Drycleaners." But Briggs also tells us that Bogeys are

> extremely quiet in their movements and in their voices. They never shout and they speak in gentle voices scarcely above a whisper.
>
> Perhaps this is because a lot of their normal aggression is dissipated at work.
>
> At home, they are gentle, shy, and very polite to one another. So . . . .
>
> BE QUIET WHILE YOU READ THIS BOOK. (5)

Nothing here seems calculated to appeal to low childish tastes—on the contrary. And there are numerous other references to Bogey gentleness and love of quiet. Bogey bicycles have "soft, fat tires (for slowness)" (8). A favorite Bogey sport is tiddlywinks, "probably because it is silent and requires no exertion. As with most Bogey games, the object is to achieve a draw" (13). The favorite spectator sport is Bogeyball, a relative of soccer, whose aim is

> To put the ball into the player's own goal and help the opposing team to put the ball into their goal. . . . Should two players accidentally bump into one another, they will immediately step back and bow formally, emitting a quiet hiss at the same time. . . .
>
> Bogeymen never run or hurry, not even in their games, so the match proceeds with an almost dream-like slow motion.
>
> There is no shouting or cheering. The crowd expresses its approval with quiet hissing. A goal is greeted with complete silence and stillness; many spectators instantly fall asleep. (22)

Not even at work does Fungus display real aggression. Stolidly going through the motions of a monster, he wonders whether there is much point in scaring people: "'I wonder if it does *them* any good? . . . I can't think what else I could do. . . . I'm quite happy, really. It's just that I'd like to know WHY . . .'" (17 and 20). Such thoughtfulness also seems characteristic of Bogey nature. Bogey graffiti, for example, "is never scatological. It almost always consists of platitudes or grave philosophical statements." "Silence is deep as eternity—speech is shallow as time," reads one typical inscription (9).

Bogeydom is not simply our world turned upside-down. Bogeymen lead lives much like ours; they have families, sleep in beds, use bathrooms, play tiddlywinks, and so on. It is the Bogey value system that stands in radical opposition to our own—not only in matters of hygiene, but in its concept of what the quality of life should be. Through this opposition, Briggs makes of *Fungus* both a plea for tolerance and understanding of creatures different from ourselves, and a critique of our own civilization.

Form reinforces content in eliciting tolerance. The strip-format itself, as well as Briggs's own idiosyncratic deviations from it, must be tolerated, or we cannot even approach the book and its world. Then, the minimal storyline is interrupted so continually by notes, diagrams, and explanations that our reading rate slackens almost to the dreamlike pace of life in Bogeydom; Briggs coaxes the reader to slow down, to look closely, to reflect on unfamiliar mores. Finally, the scientific detachment of the anonymous narrator helps us maintain a kind of emotional neutrality and objectivity toward the subject matter. We are asked neither to identify with Fungus nor to feel disgust at him, only to observe and to learn.

This process of adjustment may be different for adults and children. Adult readers are more likely to be repelled by Bogey love of filth and attracted by Bogey quietness, gentleness, and love of literature. For young readers, an initial attraction to Bogeys as taboo-breakers may help them accept Bogey quietness, slowness, lack of aggression, and fondness for "grave philosophical statements." For both, something alien must be accepted along with what is more naturally congenial. And acceptance gradually becomes understanding, even affection. It is impossible to finish the book—if one can finish it—without some fondness for the melancholy Fungus and this race of shy, homely creatures with "very small tops to their heads" (29).

By using imaginary beings, rather than some distant human tribe, Briggs universalizes the theme of tolerance. Bogeymen may be interpreted as another social class, another ethnic group, or another species altogether. The other-species possibility is emphasized by the chart of Bogey anatomy, which reveals the Bogeyman's long, coiled tongue ("used for catching flies"), vestigial spinal fin, three nipples, and four stomachs. ("They constantly regurgitate their food and rechew it, in the manner of Surface cows" [18].) At the same time, their more-or-less human clothing and way of life encourage us to interpret the Bogeymen as a different race or (literally) lower social class. Particularly the latter. Bogeydom, from what we see of it, is exclusively a working-class world, with no professions beyond those of policeman and librarian. The Bogeymen bicycling up the tunnels to the Surface from their drab rows of houses look very much like a crowd of working men on their way to the factory, while their recreations (pub games, holiday camps, Bogeyball) are those associated with the British lower classes. Raymond Briggs himself came from a working-class family, and there is at least one similarity between Fungus and Briggs's milkman father; both have a "round" of houses to which they deliver their stock-in-trade while most of their customers are still asleep.

Briggs's plea for tolerance is interwoven with his critique of modern civilization. First, we are forced to realize that Bogeymen are no more repulsive to us than we are to them. We learn, for example, that Bogey horror films feature "Sunlight, flowers, cornfields, and hot dry beaches with Drycleaners laughing gaily and playing loud music" (25). Teenage rebellion in Bogeydom is linked to an unhealthy preoccupation with the ways of humankind:

> These "drop-ins" also profess to like bright colours and noise. Ancient gramophone recordings and abandoned equipment have been smuggled in from Surface rubbish dumps and these are used with a total disregard for tradition, custom, and even law. Worse still, some of the more extreme members of the cult began keeping themselves clean, scraping off their protective layers of dirt and slime and taking baths in warm, clean water. (25)

We are even shown pages from *Where to Watch Drycleaners: A Field Guide to Surface Life*, in which we find ourselves described as creatures with "Tiny, malformed ears and tiny noses" and "Minute mouths with thick pink lips," who breed "in noisy, very crowded colonies. Easily located by noise and smell" (37).

Seen through Bogey eyes, Drycleaner civilization seems loud, shallow, contentious, restless, and horrifyingly violent. For Bogeys hurt no living creature. Their version of "pig-sticking" consists of sticking pigs to walls with muck to see how long they will stay there (12). Their only guns are wooden ones— "found to be much more satisfactory, as they are silent and harmless" (13). One cannot even hold the boils against them, for Bogeys *like* boils. It is ironic, Briggs implies, that we are so repelled by dirt and smelliness and other natural aspects of our own bodies— and so little disturbed by the noise and destruction and brutal aggressiveness of our world.

The double theme in *Fungus* of tolerance for other creatures and cultures and self-criticism of our own provides a key to other picture books. In his early *Jim and the Beanstalk*, for example, Briggs radically alters the values of the folktale. The boy Jim does not steal the old giant's possessions, but procures him a wig, spectacles, and set of false teeth, renewing his youth and spirits. Like the Bogeymen, the giant seems to represent a class, race, or species that has been exploited or misunderstood. *Jim and the Beanstalk* suggests that we can, with fairness and compassion, rewrite the old tale of our own history and repair the injustices done by a former generation.

Father Christmas, too, presents a version of contemporary society that has achieved a kind of harmony and equality between classes. The first of Briggs's strip-format books, it depicts Father Christmas as a lower-class hero based openly on the artist's milkman father. "I used to watch him and listen to him get ready to make his rounds," Briggs recalls (Mercier 12). His Christmas Eve round binds together every home he visits, from the humble trailer to Buckingham Palace. Like Briggs's father, he works long, cold hours and grumbles constantly (Mercier 12), yet he can enjoy wholeheartedly the creature comforts of a good dinner, "nice clean socks," and the "lovely" brandy set out for him by a considerate customer. The final frames, which show him presenting a gaily-wrapped fish and bone to his own cat and dog, confirm the meaningfulness of his role.

A sequel, *Father Christmas Goes on Holiday* (1975), cheerfully admits some characteristic limitations of that same working class Briggs had canonized in *Father Christmas*. Despite his desire for an exotic getaway, Father Christmas proves hopelessly insular and urban, unable to settle down either in France (where the food gives him indigestion), or in the Scottish Highlands (where he catches cold). At last he discovers the vacationland of his dreams—Las Vegas! But there is genuine admiration as well as lighthearted satire in Briggs's depiction of American society at its most extravagant. As a recent visitor to the United States, Briggs had been struck by its friendliness and freedom from class-consciousness (Mercier 12). In the fantasy hotel called Nero's Palace, the working-class man can live like a king—till his money runs out.

Fungus the Bogeyman followed the Father Christmas books. Like *Father Christmas*, it is based on the daily routine of work, yet with an underlying sadness that is absent from the earlier story. Both end with the protagonist snug in bed, but while Father Christmas's last action is to hand out presents and wish the reader a "'Happy Blooming Christmas to you too!'" Fungus's is to question the meaning of his life. "'Why am *I* a Bogeyman?'" he demands. "'What are we frightening them for? Does it do any *ultimate good*? (or even *ultimate bad*?)'" (39). Mildew cannot understand what is troubling her husband. "'Come along, drear, better get to bed—your brain is overtired,'" she says (39). Our final glimpse of them shows her fast asleep, while Fungus lies staring out of the page at us with a great black question mark over his green head. "And so," reads the caption, "we say Farewell to Fungus as he lies awake pondering upon The Significance of His Role in Society, Evolution and LIFE" (40). Over the bed a framed quotation from Swinburne reads, "Even the weariest river/ Winds somewhere safe to sea"—referring (as in its original context) to death as readily as to sleep.

In *Fungus*, for the first time, Briggs seems doubtful about the direction of modern society, and in particular the fate of those who have no control over it. Bogeydom is at once immune to some conspicuous ills of our civilization, and prone to others. Fungus's sense of purposelessness and alienation is what, for some, defines twentieth-century humanity. Like many in the post-industrial age, he can no longer find meaning in what he does for a living, only in his family relationships and leisure

activities. He can look forward only to the annihilation of his
individuality in death.   Briggs assigns no blame for this
situation—not yet; the gentle society Fungus belongs to seems
less responsible than his own gloomy temperament, which
seems to echo that of his creator. When Elaine Moss asked him
about the character of Fungus, Briggs responded, "I'm noticing
all my characters now are sad old men or, rather, sad middle-
aged men, which is what I am probably" (28).

Briggs's next picture book, *The Snowman* (1978), was in
some ways a reaction from *Fungus the Bogeyman*. Briggs himself
has confessed that the reason it contains no text is because he
was so tired of hand-lettering long captions ("Boston" 96–7). It is
a pleasant, fanciful story, again in strip-format, aimed more
accessibly at a younger audience, about a snowman who comes
to life in the night, makes friends with the little boy who created
him, and takes him on a magical flight to the seaside. There is no
hint of social criticism. Though snowman and boy belong to
different realms, they can (unlike Bogeymen and Drycleaners)
communicate and have fun together. Like a Bogeyman, the
snowman enters and explores a human home while its owners
are asleep, but as the welcome guest of his young friend.

The ending, however, is as melancholy as the ending of
Fungus; when the boy wakes up the next morning, the snowman
has melted down to a featureless little heap and is gone forever.
There is a strong contrast with the ending of *Jim and the Beanstalk*,
also the story of a boy's friendship with an alien being; unlike
the snowman, the giant survives—and, thanks to Jim, happier
and healthier than before. Yet again, as in *Fungus*, no blame can
be assigned for what is, after all, the natural fate of snowmen.
Sorrow, in both stories, is accepted as an inevitable condition of
our existence.

The Snowman has become Briggs's most commercially
successful picture book. Its theme of a friendship that crosses
natural barriers, terminated only by death—as in *Charlotte's
Web*—has a strong appeal for children. The snowman himself, at
once large and cuddly, paternal and childlike, like a giant teddy
bear, is more fun to have around than the grumpy Father
Christmas or the gloomy Fungus; it makes sense that he
eventually took the form of a plush toy. There are *Snowman*

dishes, *Snowman* Christmas cards, and a prizewinning *Snowman* video which captures to an unusual degree the beauty and wonder of the original.[3]

Yet Raymond Briggs's next strip-format picture book, *Gentleman Jim* (1980), takes a sudden downturn. Here Briggs returns to his concern with modern society, but the indirect critique of *Fungus* has become a diatribe. Jim is a Walter Mittyish little lavatory attendant (like Fungus, literally an *untermensch*), none too bright and bullied by every authority figure he encounters. Enacting his dream of a more exciting and fulfilling job, he becomes a highwayman, and despite his obvious harmlessness is promptly thrown into prison, where he ends up once more cleaning the communal toilets. No one, save his equally childlike wife Hilda and, in a single frame, a bookseller, shows him compassion, or even tolerance—not even his next-door neighbors.

"'I got ideas above my station,'" Jim says humbly on the final page, confessing the unforgivable. In a world in which wealth, social standing, and academic qualifications are prerequisites for all the worthwhile jobs, the poor, the weak, and the ignorant must be forced ruthlessly into the niches that no one else wants. In a world so rigidly bureaucratic that Jim cannot put a donkey in his yard without getting into trouble with four different officials, the poor, the weak, and the ignorant are likely to run afoul of the law as well. If they dare to dream of being Gentlemen, they must be cruelly punished for it.

From the existential melancholy of *Fungus*, Briggs has descended to total pessimism. The only mitigating factor in Jim's life is the love between him and Hilda, and in the end they are separated by prison bars. Yet there is an even darker level, an ultimate failure of humanity, that Briggs feels compelled to explore.

On the cover of each of his picture books since *Father Christmas* is a full frontal, waist-length portrait of its chief character, and through these portraits, we can trace the philosophical progress of his work. Father Christmas looks tough, sturdy, self-respecting, and, in *Father Christmas Goes on Holiday*, happy. Fungus, on the other hand, looks sad and a little foolish with his tiny, close-set eyes and wide, down-curving mouth, despite his bulky body and powerful hands. The snowman's mouth curves upward in a smile, but his almost featureless round face and sloping shoulders also make him seem innocent and helpless, foreshadowing his final fate. Jim's portrait, which shows him at work in the lavatory, marks the next stage. Like all these characters, he is rounded in shape, but to even greater extremes. His face has become a perfect circle with tiny, sad features and a few frail wisps of hair; set next to officials, he is only half their size. The confidence and strength of character that enabled Father Christmas to cope with the modern world have entirely disappeared.

The cover of Briggs's 1982 picture book *When the Wind Blows* departs slightly from the established pattern, featuring not one character but three—the small, round Jim and Hilda and in the background, looming powerfully over them, a huge mushroom cloud.

When the Wind Blows began with a classified 1980 British government pamphlet entitled *Protect and Survive*, which suggested that if simple protective measures were taken, the population could survive a nuclear war. When the contents of the pamphlet were leaked, the public was outraged. E.P. Thompson, a historian and critic of British nuclear policy, responded with a book called *Protest and Survive*, which became a rallying cry for the peace movement. Raymond Briggs's response was to imagine what would happen to Jim and Hilda in a nuclear holocaust.

At first, the couple are only mildly worried by the prospect of war. In their sixties, they remember World War II, and expect to muddle through the next one in much the same way. They pay dutiful attention to the radio broadcasts, construct their makeshift fallout shelter according to the instructions in government pamphlets, survive the blast in it, and, in the last few pages, die slowly of radiation sickness. The book alternates between strip-format scenes of the couple at home, bewildered yet optimistic, and double-page spreads of the juggernaut planes, ships, and bombs that are being unleashed upon them. This is Briggs's final indictment of our society—that it has betrayed these little people, who will go on trusting it to the end.

Gentleman Jim was sold as a children's book, probably out of habit, because Briggs had become known for his children's books, and this one looked at first glance like the rest. Clearly, this was a mistake. Even the older children who enjoy *Fungus* will not appreciate Briggs's satirization of bureaucratic institutions which they are scarcely aware of, or the savage irony of the ending. *When the Wind Blows*, even more obviously a picture book for adults, was marketed as such, selling widely to an audience who knew nothing of Briggs's children's books. Adapted by Briggs into a one-act play in 1983, it was produced in Bristol and in London, to equally powerful effect.[4] In moving from the hopefulness of *Jim and the Beanstalk* to the pessimism of *Gentleman Jim* and *When the Wind Blows*, Raymond Briggs had precisely demarcated a boundary between books for children and books for adults. It lay somewhere between *Fungus the Bogeyman* and *Gentleman Jim*—between an imaginary society gentler than our own and a real society seen through the eyes of its oppressed—and especially, between sorrow and despair.[5]

NOTES

1. For a discussion of the strip-format genre from a publisher's perspective, see James Bruce, "New and Different: The Strip-Format Book."

2. See, for example, Louise Seaman Bechtel, "The Comics and Children's Books." Maurice Sendak has brought a degree of acceptance in America to the strip-format book with such picture books as *In the Night Kitchen* (1970). Overall, however, Sendak's strip-format looks much less like a comic book than Briggs's does.

3. Perry Nodelman discusses *The Snowman* in detail in *Words About Pictures: The Narrative Art of Children's Picture Books*. In "The Film of the Picture Book: Raymond Briggs's *The Snowman* as Progressive and Regressive Texts," Geoff Moss argues that the differences between the book and the film are great enough to produce works that are in ideological opposition to each other; the book is "progressive" and "potentially subversive," while the film is "regressive in the way in

which it carefully neutralizes criticism of the social order and reproduces the conditions of its own production" (195).

4. Excerpts from reviews of the London production of *When the Wind Blows* are printed on the back cover of the published script. *The Times* called the performance an "unforgettable theatrical experience"; the *Observer* "irresistible . . . possibly the most bizarre theatre I have seen"; and the *Daily Express* "one of the most disturbingly real events I have experienced inside a theatre." Adapted as a radio play, *When the Wind Blows* won an award for most outstanding radio program from the Broadcasting Press Guild in 1983. *Gentleman Jim* was also produced as a play, in 1985.

5. Raymond Briggs has, as of 1993, seemingly abandoned his career as a children's writer. A later strip-format book, *The Tin Pot Foreign General and the Old Iron Woman* (1984), followed the pattern we have already seen with *Gentleman Jim* and *When the Wind Blows*. The story is a savage satire on the Falklands War—the Old Iron Woman being, of course, the British Prime Minister, Margaret Thatcher. Like *Gentleman Jim* and *When the Wind Blows*, it makes no pretense of being accessible to children; familiarity with the events and controversial nature of the war is necessary to make sense of what is going on in the picture book, and to account for its tone of unmodulated anger.

WORKS CITED

Bechtel, Louise Seaman. "The Comics and Children's Books." *Horn Book* 17, 4 (July 1941): 296–303.

Briggs, Katharine. *An Encyclopedia of Fairies, Hobgoblins, Brownies, Bogies, and Other Supernatural Creatures*. New York: Pantheon, 1976.

Briggs, Raymond. "Boston Globe-Horn Book Award Acceptance Speech." *Horn Book* 56, 1 (Feb 1980): 96–7.

———. *Father Christmas*. Harmondsworth: Puffin Books, 1973.

———. *Father Christmas Goes on Holiday*. Harmondsworth: Puffin Books, 1975.

———. *Fungus the Bogeyman*. New York: Random House, 1979.

———. *Gentleman Jim*. London: Hamish Hamilton, 1980.

————. *Jim and the Beanstalk*. New York: Coward, McCann and Geoghegan, 1970.

————. *The Snowman*. New York: Random House, 1978.

————. *The Tin Pot General and the Old Iron Woman*. New York: Little, Brown, 1984.

————. *When the Wind Blows*. New York: Schocken Books, 1982.

————. *When the Wind Blows*. (Dramatic adaptation.) London: Samuel French, 1983.

Bruce, James. "New and Different: The Strip-Format Book." *Notes from Delacorte Press Books for Young Readers* (Winter 1980/Spring 1981): 6–7.

Chambers, Aidan. "Letter from England: *Fungus* Encore." *Horn Book* 56, 1 (Feb 1980): 99–103.

Mercier, Jean F. "PW Interviews: Raymond Briggs." *Publisher's Weekly*, 5 November 1973: 12–13.

Moss, Elaine. "Raymond Briggs: On British Attitudes to the Strip Cartoon and Children's-Book Illustration." *Signal* 31 (January 1979): 28–31.

Moss, Geoff. "The Film of the Picture Book: Raymond Briggs's *The Snowman* as Progressive and Regressive Texts." *Children's Literature in Education* 22, 3 (September 1991): 195–204.

Nodelman, Perry. *Words About Pictures: The Narrative Art of Children's Picture Books*. Athens, Georgia: University of Georgia Press, 1988.

Vaccine for Future Shock: Diana Wynne Jones

> Time City was in upheaval all around them as they went
> down the steps. . . . The steps heaved under them with
> long shudders, and cracks appeared under their feet. In
> the distance, people were running across the Avenue of
> the Four Ages, in order to get to the river and escape, and
> Vivian did not blame them. A particularly grinding
> shudder produced a long crashing, over to her right. She
> looked in time to see the golden Dome of The Years slide
> away sideways and disappear in a great billow of dust.
> One of the metal arches in the Avenue tipped crooked,
> and beyond that, with a mighty tinkling, the blue glass
> dome of Millennium crumbled down on itself and poured
> blue shards into the River Time.
>
> Diana Wynne Jones, *A Tale of Time City*

Modern fantasy begins at the turn of our century, with E. Nesbit. One particular variety that has been popular with three generations of children's writers was virtually her creation— those stories in which the primary setting is our own twentieth-century world, and the protagonists ordinary children like ourselves.[1] Into this world, magic unexpectedly intrudes and must be dealt with, usually without the help of adults.

In E. Nesbit's prototype, *Five Children and It* (1902), four brothers and sisters (the fifth child is their baby brother, the Lamb) find a magical creature in the sandpit near their summer home. The Psammead—or "Sand Fairy"—has the power of giving wishes, and allows them one wish a day, whose effects will be canceled out at sunset. The children discover by experience the boobytraps in wishes for beauty, wealth, being "bigger," making their baby brother grow up, and bringing their favorite adventure stories to life. They learn to word their wishes carefully and consider logical consequences—though someone is always carelessly saying "I wish—" and bringing on another catastrophe. In the end they decide of their own accord to wish that the Psammead be unable to grant them wishes any longer. A Victorian fantasist would have treated the theme of wish-fulfillment with stern didacticism—as Jean Ingelow does in "The Ouphe of the Wood" and Juliana Ewing in "Melchior's Dream." E. Nesbit brings out its comic side. Each foolish wish sets off a funny and suspenseful adventure, and we are less inclined to feel superior to the four children for their heedlessness than to admire their ingenuity under stress.

Magic is treacherous in *The Five Children and It*, but in later E. Nesbit fantasies it becomes a force which can, to a limited extent, be mastered and used to good ends. In *The Story of the Amulet*, the four children acquire a broken but still magical amulet with the power to take them time traveling in search of its missing half. The whole amulet can restore their mother, convalescing in Madeira, and their father, who has been sent to Manchuria as a war correspondant. Toward this goal, the children are determined to "work" their amulet "for all it's worth" (196). This means understanding not only how the amulet operates, but the laws governing time itself. At one point, for example, Cyril theorizes that by traveling into the future instead of the past, they can learn when and where they *will* have found the missing half. "And then we can go back and do the finding really" (221). Though his ploy fails, it is an impressive piece of reasoning that yields helpful information. Eventually, the children do find the whole amulet, and their parents return safe and sound. In *The Enchanted Castle* (1907), a group of children learn similarly how to deal with a wishing ring. In *The Magic City* (1910), Philip and Lucy come to grips with a whole magical kingdom and its idiosyncratic natural laws. E. Nesbit encourages children to believe that they can enter a strange new situation, learn its rules, and then use their knowledge to attain their goals. She takes for granted a world in which the rules will go on working indefinitely, once you have mastered them—a world whose future is predictable and stable.

The E. Nesbit-type fantasy is still a favorite with children's authors, but the world she knew vanished in the smoke and poison gas of World War I. Change, in our century, seems increasingly rapid and all-encompassing. There is no area of life—from cosmology to dating customs—in which the old rules still work as they once did, and no assurance that the rules we use now will last.

This is the reality reflected in fantasy by Diana Wynne Jones. Her variations on the E. Nesbit tradition might be called "postmodern," not because the characters listen to rock music and come from broken families, but in the quality of the magic itself. Learning the rules, in a Diana Wynne Jones fantasy, does not ensure mastery. Rules change without warning; basic assumptions turn upside-down; the world itself may be unstable, shifting between alternate versions of reality, or tilting toward total chaos. Adaptability becomes a survival characteristic—as it is today. Jones writes for today's children, who face a future no one can foresee. Complex in structure, intellectually challenging, often bewildering, her fantasies are a kind of vaccine for future shock.

Yet she will not allow adaptability to become an end in itself. Jones has deep roots in the realm of myth and myth's unchanging realities; she assumes the ultimate moral responsibility of the individual, and the ability to discern moral truth even in a chaotic world. There is a cosmic harmony toward which her characters are called to strive, though the earth may be crumbling beneath their feet. If E. Nesbit is one important predecessor for her, so is J.R.R. Tolkien, and his image of Frodo wrestling with Gollum at the Cracks of Doom.[2]

Themes later developed with more depth and complexity are present even in her earliest fantasies for children, *Witch's Business* (originally published in England in 1973 as *Wilkins' Tooth*) and *The Ogre Downstairs* (1974). Of the two, the latter belongs most obviously to the E. Nesbit tradition. Caspar, Johnny, and their younger sister Gwinny acquire a magical chemistry set which allows them to perform experiments with flying, invisibility, making inanimate objects come alive, and so on; each experiment leads to humorous misadventures, as they attempt to conceal the results from their parents, and they are more relieved than sorry when the magic chemicals are gone. To this extent, *The Ogre Downstairs* is very like *Five Children and It*— the flying episode, especially, seems inspired by the Five Children's wish for "wings."

But Jones, already experimenting, has crossbred the traditional wish-fulfillment fantasy with the family story of the 1970s. The mother has recently remarried, and her husband—the Ogre, as the three children secretly call him—has two sons of his own; mutual hostilities within the new family are running high. This situation compounds the misadventures—there are actually two chemistry sets operating independently, as the Ogre has given his sons a set too—yet in the end, magical misadventure unites the ill-assorted septet. One turning point comes when Caspar and Malcolm inadvertently trade bodies for a day and gain some understanding of each other. Another occurs when Gwinny tries to kill the Ogre with a poisoned cake, but realizes in time that he is not such a bad person after all. Such moments of illumination—of realizing how wrongly one has judged someone else—were to become characteristic of Jones's work, as was her concern with difficult family relationships.

In *The Ogre Downstairs*, magic is localized within the family, as it is in *Five Children and It*, and carries no dangerous implications. (We cannot really believe in Gwinny's resolve to kill the Ogre.) The worst possible outcome for this story would be disintegration of the newly-formed family into its original components.

In *Witch's Business*, the stakes are much higher. The opening premise seems harmless enough: Jess and Frank, desperate for money, invent Own Back Ltd, which specializes in arranged revenges. It's the kind of money-making scheme a child might really come up with; as a child, Jones came up with it herself (see her comment on the dust jacket). To their astonishment, however, Jess and Frank find themselves in an increasingly complex and nasty mess. To begin with, their personal enemy, the local bully and gang-leader Buster Knell, forces them to obtain one of Vernon Wilkins' teeth, as compensation for the tooth Wilkins has knocked out in a fight with him. Then Martin Taylor wants his Own Back on the Adams girls, who call him names, and the Adams girls want their Own Back on old Biddy Iremonger, who they insist has given Jenny a limp and stolen the family treasure.

Vernon persuades Jess and Frank to give Buster a baby tooth from his little brother Silas instead—it is, after all, still "Wilkins' tooth"—but Buster takes the tooth to Biddy Iremonger, and soon poor Silas' face is "blown out like a balloon" (40). Biddy Iremonger, it seems, is a witch, and nothing the children can offer will induce her to return the tooth, put Silas' face back to normal, or heal Jenny Adams's foot.

She "has it in for" the Adams family, she tells Jess. And besides, "'You've been trespassing on my business, haven't you? You and your brother. I'll have you know that Own Back is my concern, not yours . . .'" (49). Ire-mongering is, literally, a witch's business.

When Jess and Frank discover that Buster and his gang have sold themselves to Biddy Iremonger in return for her tooth spell, they begin to realize how self-destructive Own Back can be. "'You've been meddling with people's worse natures, haven't you?'" a mysterious lady warns Jess. When Jess reluctantly admits that they have, the lady gives her a charm against the Evil Eye (71–2). The attempt to retrieve Wilkins' tooth has become a struggle with evil itself.

The children are able to defeat Biddy Iremonger only by renouncing Own Back—by burying their feuds and joining forces. Jess, Frank, Martin, the Adams sisters, Vernon Wilkins, even Buster and his gang, now desperate to free themselves from her, all converge on Biddy's hut and seize the tooth. Although she takes them prisoner, they succeed in hiding the tooth from her, passing it back and forth to each other like a game of Hide the Thimble and refusing, under great pressure, to give it up. Once united and mutually supportive, the children find themselves stronger and more resourceful than a cruel and immensely powerful adult. And in the end, Jess finds a stratagem that destroys Biddy and her spells together.

The greater moral seriousness of *Witch's Business*, underlying what children would call simply a funny and exciting story, points in the direction of Jones's later, deeper fantasy. The magic, however, here and in *The Ogre Downstairs*, still looks back toward the E. Nesbit tradition. Once you know the rules, you can predict, outwit, even control the supernatural. The supernatural itself tends to be limited and concrete. In *The Ogre Downstairs*, magic is measured in test-tubes; once identified, a magical "chemical" can be administered in precisely controlled doses, or counteracted with an antidote. When a tube of "Dens Drac." is spilled by mistake and armed warriors start popping out of the pavement, the Ogre, who knows "'the old trick'" (184), incites them to attack each other by hurling cans into their midst, Cadmus-style. The more powerful magic of *Witch's Business* also adheres to familiar, very concrete rules: possession of Silas's tooth gives Biddy the power to hurt him by the magical "law of contagion," while the charm against the Evil Eye repels Buster's gang like an electric fence. Like the Ogre, Jess remembers an "old trick"; she persuades Biddy to demonstrate her powers to the captive children by changing into a mouse, which is promptly devoured by her own feline familiar.

It seems too trite and easy a solution. Biddy, as she has been portrayed, is crafty as well as ruthless, hardly the type to be taken in so readily, even if she has never happened to hear "Puss in Boots." The magic works too predictably to be dramatically satisfying.

But *Witch's Business* was the last of Jones's conventional fantasies. By the end of 1975, her work had taken its postmodern turn; all three of the full-length fantasies published that year—*Eight Days of Luke*, *Cart and Cwidder*, and *Dogsbody*—each quite different from the others, feature a new, deeper, more pervasive and complex magic with rules by no means easy to discern. Each of her protagonists finds his basic judgments and assumptions utterly mistaken. And each discovers that his decisions may affect not merely his family, or a small group of acquaintances, but the fate of a kingdom—a planet—even a universe. They have entered mythical territory, where tragedy becomes possible—yet without leaving comedy behind. Whatever their new depth and complexity, Jones's fantasies continue to fulfill her "first aim" as an author: "to make a story—as amusing and exciting as possible—such as I wished I could have read as a child" (*Something* 117).

Her second aim, she says, is to give children "the benefit of my greater experience" in "the private terrors and troubles" they suffer through.

> Children create about a third of their misery themselves. The other two-thirds is caused by adults—inconsiderate, mysterious, and often downright frightening adults. I put adults like this in my stories, in some firmly contemporary situation beset with very real problems, and explore the implications by means of magic and old myths. What I am after is an exciting—and exacting—wisdom, in which contemporary life and potent myth are intricately involved and superimposed. I would like children to discover that potent old truths are as much part of everyone's daily life as are—say—the days of the week.

She might well be describing *Eight Days of Luke*, the 1975 fantasy which shows most clearly her transition from conventional beginnings to a realm of fantasy unmistakably her own. It is a more lighthearted book than *Cart and Cwidder* or *Dogsbody*, and still slightly reminiscent of E. Nesbit. Like the Five Children, David is starting his summer holidays when magic unexpectedly enters, disrupts, and transforms his life.

The adults David lives with—great-Aunt Dot, Great-Uncle Bernard, Cousin Ronald, and Ronald's wife Cousin Astrid—are not actually cruel, only utterly, selfishly uninterested in him. They decide to pack him off to a math tutor for the holidays, just to get him out of the house. Furious, David resolves to put a curse on *their* holidays, and declaims strange syllables at random. Suddenly, something works. The garden wall collapses, the heaving earth bursts into flame and erupts with giant serpents, and a freckled, red-headed, laughing stranger appears from nowhere. As he and David battle the serpents together, and slam them underground again with garden spades, they instantly become friends.

Luke, as the stranger calls himself, seems only slightly older than David. He keeps insisting how much he owes David for releasing him from prison—which David's "curse" has apparently achieved. He can play cricket, perform all kinds of mischievous, entertaining tricks with fire, and charm David's relatives besides.

At first, David is simply delighted with his new friend. But when Luke sets an office building on fire to amuse him, he feels "itchy and guilty" (58), and makes Luke put it out. He begins to suspect that "Luke did not operate by the same rules as other people" and that, "if so, Luke was something of a responsibility" (61–2). Two more mysterious strangers turn up, in pursuit of Luke—first the brutish Mr. Chew, then the pleasant, keen-eyed Mr. Wedding with his pair of ravens—and David instinctively helps Luke escape. Yet when Mr. Wedding tells him that Luke was put in prison for doing "'something very terrible'" (88), and that "'he took a revenge on us from prison which has had serious consequences already and is going to have worse'" (89), David cannot help believing it. At this point, though he still refuses to betray Luke and does not know who Mr. Wedding's "us" refers to, he is no longer sure of being on the right side.

At some point, the young reader must realize who all these mysterious people are—Luke, Mr. Chew, Mr. Wedding, the "tall man with red-fair hair" (110) who shows up on Thursday, the huge, blond, genial Mr. and Mrs. Fry, even Mr. Wedding's "lady chauffeur" (82). Jones drops a broad hint or two— "'Funny,'" jokes David, "'. . . that Mr. Chew turned up on Chewsday'" (70)—and even today's children have probably been told at some point that the days of the week were called after Norse gods. Typically, however, Jones names no names till very near the end of the book (169), encouraging readers to make the discovery for themselves. The more they happen to know of Norse myth, the more they will enjoy how ingeniously she has superimposed it on the banal foreground of our own world.

But the discovery that solves the puzzle also uncovers a moral dilemma of cosmic magnitude. If Luke is Loki and Mr. Wedding Odin, there is no question of which is the "right" side. In the struggle of chaos to destroy creation, Loki is aligned with the forces of evil, and Odin with those of good. Luke's "revenge," which has had such "serious consequences," was to hide Thor's hammer, Miolnir, a weapon badly needed for the coming battle of Ragnarok. He must be made to tell where the hammer is. Yet to help the gods recapture and re-imprison him is still, for David, to betray a friend.

David, a naturally thoughtless boy, grows to meet the challenge. He resists Mr. Wedding's efforts to bribe, threaten, and out-argue him, winning Mr. Wedding's respect in the process. Finally, he agrees to try to find the hammer, in exchange for Luke's freedom—a bargain that benefits both the gods and his friend. His success brings the story to a triumphant close, and with an unexpected bonus for himself. During the tumultuous "eight days of Luke," he has been learning to like Cousin Astrid, while she has been jolted out of her own boredom and hypochondria and become his ally. He returns from recovering Miolnir to find that Great-Aunt Dot, Great-Uncle Bernard, and Cousin Ronald, who have been milking his inheritance, have been exposed (with a little help from Mr. Wedding) and forced to flee the country—leaving him free to set up a much happier home with Astrid.

Eight Days of Luke makes an imaginative and ambitious attempt to combine the fun, suspense, and contemporary realism of an E. Nesbit-type fantasy with the "potent old truths" of Norse myth—and almost succeeds. One problem is David's relatives, who (excepting Astrid) are such caricatures that we cannot take his family problems seriously. And superimposing Norse myth on this comic-book milieu is like decanting old wine into a new bottle slightly too small for it. The power and stark tragedy essential to this mythic world will not fit; even David's quest for the hammer is less thrilling and dangerous than it should be. Jones was to be more successful as she took to inventing more of the mythology herself.

What works in *Eight Days of Luke* is the way in which discovery creates a reversal of assumptions. Along with David, we initially accept Luke as a friend. When other characters appear in pursuit of him—when we see his fear of them, hear how harshly they have treated him, and join David in outwitting them—we classify them automatically as antagonists—the "bad guys." Learning who all these people really are and what is at stake turns our classifications upside-down. We have been rooting enthusiastically for the wrong team. Even more disconcertingly, Luke is not simply Evil, and David cannot simply stop liking him. When David finally realizes who Luke is, "he knew . . . he would never be able to think of Luke in the same way again" (167). But he also discovers that "knowing all about someone need not change your feelings at all" (168), and that he and Luke are still friends.

It is this kind of complexity that makes Jones "postmodern" as a writer of fantasy. David has to keep his mental and moral balance even as he begins to see how wrong he has been. His success is the measure of his willingness to accept a new version of reality, and his ability to discern and follow his own course through the midst of it.

Both *Dogsbody* and *Cart and Cwidder*, Jones's other 1975 fantasies, incorporate the same concept, though in quite different ways. The protagonist of *Dogsbody* is a luminary, the immortal guardian of the star Sirius. As the story opens, he has just been found guilty of murdering a fellow luminary with an instrument of power called a Zoi—which has disappeared somewhere on the planet Earth. His punishment is to be reborn in the body of a dog. If he can find the missing Zoi, he will be restored to his old place in the heavens; otherwise, he will live and die an animal. Sirius, as it happens, is innocent, but too angry and confused to defend himself effectively. The next thing he knows, he is a newborn puppy, with no memory of his former identity. As in *Eight Days of Luke*, the plot develops from the search for a missing object of power, but Sirius is so much more handicapped than David and has so much more to lose that his situation grips the reader far more powerfully. His slow awakening of consciousness within the alien body, and his experience of a dog's world are brilliantly handled. And his evolving relationship with Kathleen, the girl who rescues him as a drowning puppy, raises him, and loves him with all her heart, has an emotional depth beyond anything in Jones's earlier novels.

For Sirius, what overturns his assumptions is the discovery that his beloved Companion, the small white luminary who accompanied him in the heavens, has hated him all along. That it was she who stole the Zoi and killed the luminary with it, she who conspired to frame him at the trial—and she who has taken human form on Earth to hunt him down and kill him. Only a dog's experience of human nature enables him to see the truth about her. And that shattering moment of revelation has wide-reaching implications. Fleeing from his Companion, Sirius takes refuge in a fox's hole, where he encounters Earth—the "beautiful and kindly" (160) planet that has nurtured him since his new birth, but whose presence he has never recognized until now. As they speak together, he realizes that Earth "contained half the universe and had taught him everything he knew" (160). By relinquishing a love based on illusion, Sirius begins to understand the reality of his adopted world, the value of his dog nature—and the meaning of his past. The trial we witnessed in the opening pages takes on an entirely different aspect for us too, as we come to see the "friend" as an enemy and the "enemies" as friends.

In *Cart and Cwidder*, the first novel of a trilogy centered in the imaginary kingdom of Dalemark, Clennan the Singer and his minstrel family travel from South to North Dalemark, secretly bearing the tidings of revolution to an oppressed people. The revelations come to Clennan's children Moril and Bird, after their father's death. Along with the reader, they learn for the first time that his career as a minstrel was only a front for his work as freedom fighter and spy—and that their widowed mother is more than willing to go home and marry her first love, a totally different kind of man. Like many children, Moril and Bird have never really known who their parents were.

This pattern—the discovery that leads to a reversal of long-held assumptions—is, of course, a very old one in literature, and Jones's extensive use of it may well owe something to the classical education she describes in "The Heroic Ideal—A Personal Odyssey." The pattern was especially prominent in Greek tragedy and is discussed in Aristotle's *Poetics*. Aristotle defines a "complex" tragic plot as one in which the change in the hero's fortunes, from good to ill or the opposite, is brought about by *anagnorisis* (the change from ignorance to knowledge, or discovery), by *peripeteia* (reversal), or by a combination of the two (*Poetics* 236). The "finest form" of *anagnorisis* is combined with *peripeteia*, as in the *Oedipus* of Sophocles (237). Aristotle goes on to list various types of *anagnorisis*—discovery by signs or marks (e.g., birthmarks), discovery "made directly by the poet," discovery through memory, discovery through reasoning, and (best of all) discovery through a "probable incident" (243–5). Sirius's discovery of his Companion's true nature, for example, occurs as a "probable incident," when he encounters and recognizes her in hostile human form, though memory and reasoning are involved as well. The main difference in Jones's use of the pattern is not that her stories have happy endings—so did many Greek tragedies—but that her *peripeteia* is less a reversal in fortune than a reversal of how the protagonist sees himself, other people, and the cosmos. The effect is disorienting not only for the protagonist but for the reader, who has shared the protagonist's assumptions about "what I am," "what they are," and "how things are."

Magic, in these later stories, resides less in objects (like a tooth or a chemistry set) than in beings. Luke can do tricks with fire because he is Loki. The protagonist's discovery of "what I really am" often involves a discovery of supernatural powers in himself. Sirius is re-discovering his lost identity as a divine luminary throughout most of *Dogsbody*. Young Moril, in *Cart and Cwidder*, learns that he alone of his siblings has inherited the ability to use the old family cwidder, a musical instrument that can literally move mountains.

This innate, even godlike magic is appropriate for stories that partake of the heroic or mythic realm, in which gods and other supernatural beings are at home. On another level, it suggests that for everyone the change from ignorance to knowledge increases both power and responsibility. Children, Jones believes, "by nature, status, and instinct, live more in the heroic mode than the rest of humanity" ("Heroic" 133), and one of her conscious aims has been to show them "how close to the old heroic ideal they so often are" ("Heroic" 134). In her fantasies, the discovery in oneself of innate supernatural power is no mere wish-fulfillment, but a metaphorical expression of the heroic potential in every child.

Since the mid-1970s, Jones has continued to weave patterns of discovery and reversal, though with such originality that each book comes as a surprise. At the same time, without losing its pace, humor, and suspense, her work has grown increasingly complex in plot and theme, making strenuous intellectual demands even on adult readers. More and more, it seems to reflect not only universal truths but the quality of life in a fast-changing, unstable world, where "reality" itself is transformed from one moment to the next.

Jones has used science fiction's concept of parallel worlds not only for its imaginative possibilities but to suggest this multiplicity of reality. In *Charmed Life* (1977), the first of her novels to feature this concept, the apprentice witch Gwendolen scribbles a hasty explanation:

> There are hundreds of other worlds only some are nicer than others, they are formed when there is a big event in History like a battle or an earthquake when the result can be two or more quite diferent [sic] things. Both those things hapen [sic] but they cannot exist together so the world splits into two worlds witch [sic] start to go diferent [sic] after that. (103)

When another "big event" happens, the world splits again, and so on, creating a whole string of parallel worlds. The main world of *Charmed Life* is parallel to ours and looks superficially like Edwardian England; its crucial difference is that magic "works" and is routinely practiced there. As soon as Gwendolen learns how to "access" parallel worlds, she moves from this world to another where she can be a queen, and is automatically replaced by a girl from the neighboring world in the series— which happens to be ours. Janet, her replacement, has to adjust to a different "reality"— one in which magic is possible.

For the reader, of course, there are added layers of complexity. After adjusting to the main world of *Charmed Life* at the beginning of the story, it is startling to encounter our world from this perspective halfway through; the familiar reality has become strange. From here on, moreover, we are experiencing the magic world from Janet's point of view, and sharing her process of adjustment. The shift back and forth between these two "realities" is dizzying, but exhilarating.

Since *Charmed Life*, Jones has written a number of parallel world fantasies. Chrestomanci, a powerful warlock in *Charmed Life*, reappears in *The Magicians of Caprona* (1980), *Witch Week* (1982), and *The Lives of Christopher Chant* (1988).[3] *Howl's Moving Castle* (1986) and *The Castle in the Air* (1990) form another pair, while *The Homeward Bounders* (1981) passes over the line from fantasy into science fiction.

In other novels, Jones creates multiple realities with time. Time City, in *A Tale of Time City* (1987), is "'built on a small patch of time and space that exists outside time and history'" (7). Here, all times exist simultaneously—all are equally "real"—and tourists from any "Stable" century (of which ours, needless to say, is not one) can come there to visit and see the sights. However, Time City itself is threatened with dissolution. History "goes critical" and begins to change, and Vivian, a girl evacuee from the London of 1939, who has come to Time City by mistake, finds that she can't get home again—the world she knew is no longer there.

The Time of the Ghost (1981) (a punning title) combines traditional materials with a startling change of perspective; instead of encountering a ghost, the protagonist *is* one. In the beginning, she has only a fragmentary memory of herself and is trying to find out who she was. She learns, eventually, that she is not dead after all, but has been in a near-fatal car accident; her ghost is revisiting the past of seven years ago in order to change it and save her life. The possibility of creating an alternative present by going back in time to correct the past is explored in several novels of this period, including *A Tale of Time City* and *Fire and Hemlock* (1985). As Jones treats it, this is no easy "second chance" for her characters, but a way of forcing them to face past mistakes honestly, and assume responsibility.

Archer's Goon (1984), yet another alternate-time story, is one I'd like to look at in detail, the better to demonstrate what kind of reading experience Jones offers. For one thing, no summary of a paragraph or two can do justice to the sheer complexity of her simplest early novels—let alone what she was up to ten years later. Of *Archer's Goon*, even the reviewer for *The Junior Bookshelf* concluded a partial synopsis with "I will say no more about the plot. To be truthful I am not sure that I understood it all" (265). Our attempt to understand *Archer's Goon* will also demonstrate how concepts and ideas first articulated in Jones's early fantasies were developed in the 1980s, and how Jones uses fantasy to express and confront the instability and confusion that today's children have inherited.

The reader's experience of *Archer's Goon* begins even before Chapter One, with the Author's Note:

This book will prove the following ten facts:

1. A Good is a being who melts into the foreground and sticks there.
2. Pigs have wings, making them hard to catch.
3. All power corrupts, but we need electricity.
4. When an irresistible force meets an immovable object, the result is a family fight.
5. Music does not always soothe the troubled breast.
6. An Englishman's home is his castle.
7. The female of the species is more deadly than the male.
8. One black eye deserves another.
9. Space is the final frontier, and so is the sewage farm.
10. It pays to increase your word power.

Most of these are familiar sayings with an unfamiliar twist. Their effect is nonsensical—note the Carrollian echo in [2]—yet with the exception of [2], each "fact" is connected to some development in the story.

The same quality of twisted familiarity permeates *Archer's Goon* from the opening sentence. "The trouble started the day Howard came home from school to find the Goon sitting in the kitchen" wraps suspense, the familiar, and the bizarre into one masterly package. The Goon is huge and smelly, with long ape-like arms and legs, enormous booted feet, a "little round fair head" with a "half-daft" expression (2), and a very sharp knife. He says that Archer has sent him to collect the two thousand words Howard's father owes him, and that he won't leave until he gets them. "A Goon is a being who melts into the foreground and sticks there." The Sykes family—consisting of Howard, his father Quentin (a writer and literature professor), his mother Catriona (a supervisor of music in schools), his aptly-nicknamed little sister Awful, and Fifi (a college student who lives with them as a mother's help)—is indeed "stuck" with him, for Quentin turns stubborn under pressure and refuses to write any words at all.

Quentin has never heard of Archer. His version is that he *has* been sending off two thousand words of "'any old thing that came into my head'" (17) every three months for the last thirteen years, but to a city official named Mountjoy, and that the arrangement was simply an idea of Mountjoy's to cure his writer's block. But Mountjoy admits that he has been forwarding the words to a "superior," one of "'the seven people who really run this town'" (26): Archer, Dillian, Venturus, Torquil, Erskine, Hathaway, and Shine. Mountjoy has never seen any of the seven in person, and has no idea which of them has been getting the words, or why anyone should want them.

It soon becomes clear, however, that Archer is not the only one who does, and the Sykeses begin to find out how formidable these "people" are. Archer, for example, as the Goon puts it, "'Farms power. . . . Gas and electricity. Money, too'" (12). It's Archer's doing when the gas and electricity are cut off and the television refuses to show anything but the words ARCHER IS WATCHING YOU. Torquil "farms" music; it's Torquil's doing when the tape deck, the television, and every instrument in the house start playing loud and discordant music at once. The gangs of older boys who attack Howard and Awful after school are from Shine, who "farms" crime. When the car won't start, it's because Hathaway "farms" transport.

Howard, Quentin, Awful, and Fifi visit Archer, who surprises them with his affability. A "big young man in overalls" (63) with a "nice, wry sort of smile" and "the bluest eyes Howard had ever seen, luminous cornflower blue" (65), he lives behind the town bank, in an airplane hanger full of machines and the latest technology. Howard, who spends every spare moment designing rocket ships, is overcome with envy. Fifi falls in love with him. But Quentin becomes increasingly dubious as Archer explains his position.

Archer hasn't been getting Quentin's words, but he badly needs to know who has. All seven of them have been inexplicably stuck inside the city boundaries for the last twenty-six years (though it feels like thirteen). Quentin's words are the one "'unusual thing'" (68) that fits the time frame. Archer has been watching Quentin for some time, through the television screen and the electric outlets, but he can't figure out what makes the words so powerful. He and Erskine also suspect that whoever is using them plans to "'get rid of us all soon'" (69) and take over the world—and Archer intends to farm the world himself, as soon as he can move on. "'I'm very fair,'" he says, "'and I'm not cruel. I'd do it well'" (94). It is Archer to whom "fact" [3] refers: "All power corrupts, but we need electricity."

As "'a taxpayer and a citizen of the world'" (72)—all seven are farming the city taxes—Quentin refuses to cooperate with Archer. When Torquil threatens Catriona with the loss of her job unless Quentin writes two thousand words for *him*, the result, as "fact" [4] puts it, is "a family fight" that goes on for days. Catriona wants Quentin to write two thousand words for Archer, and another two thousand for Torquil. Howard leans toward Quentin's side, for "though Mum and Fifi kept saying that Quentin had no right to make the rest of them suffer, Howard began to agree with Quentin more and more that you had to do a thing you knew was right, even if people did suffer" (90).

But things get much worse. The Sykeses have no heat and no gas to cook with, and are blasted with music all day long—not only from every sound apparatus they own, but from marching bands and choirs outside (see "fact" [5]). Workmen begin drilling holes in their street, filling them up, and drilling them again. They can't get money from the bank, or find a shop open to buy food (Torquil farms shops too). An enormous tax bill arrives; Quentin insists Mountjoy had told him that his two thousand words a month were paying his taxes, but now the whole thirteen years' worth has come due. The workmen drill a seven-foot-wide ditch across the front of the house. "'They say an Englishman's home is his castle!'" bawls Quentin defiantly, echoing "fact" [6]. "'Now we have a moat to prove it!'" (137). The family copes ingeniously, borrowing food from the neighbors, building campfires to cook on in the back yard, and muffling their musical instruments in sleeping bags, but their lives have become a test of endurance. The Goon suffers along with them; by now, he is almost like one of the family, and has fallen hopelessly in love with Fifi.

Howard and Awful undertake their own investigation, and manage to interview all of the seven except Erskine and Venturus. Each, they discover, has a separate domain within the town:

Archer, as we have seen, farms power and lives in an airplane hanger behind the bank. He is the eldest of the seven siblings.

Shine farms crime and lives, incongruously, in an old part of town near the cathedral, behind a school for Oriental meditation. She is a woman, which "took me aback," admits Jones ("Letter") and accounts for "fact" [7]—a "vastly fat" female of the species "dressed entirely in black leather, which made her look fatter still since the leather stretched and strained in all directions in order to get around her" (125). Her huge, dimly lit headquarter contains rows of television screens showing crimes in progress all over town, and weapons hung in "orderly hundreds" on the walls (125). Just as Howard is attracted to Archer, Awful is strongly attracted to the ruthless Shine.

Dillian farms law and order, has a "sweet, laughing" voice (45), and looks like a fairytale princess, with long golden hair, but hides a secret yen to be more like Shine herself (157). She is secretly organizing the women of the country for her own takeover. She lives in a house "like several castles melted together" (44), in an exclusive residential district. Howard is slightly bowled over by Dillian, but Awful sees through her at once.

Hathaway is markedly different from the rest. "He was quite the smallest of any of the family they had so far seen, almost normal size, in fact, probably only a few inches taller than Howard" (149). Hathaway lives in the past—in the sixteenth century, where he has a pleasant house and a wife and children. Howard and Awful find him by going through the city museum. Besides transport, he farms archives; he can tell them that the Sykeses descend from his children Anne and Will (no relation to you know who), and, more upsettingly, that Howard is adopted. Hathaway insists that he has no desire to farm the world, but has only been trying to find out what's happening, and he readily agrees to call off the road menders. Howard and Awful both like him very much.

Torquil, the fifth sibling, is tall, dark, and handsome and loves to dramatize himself, dressing in extravagant costumes. Besides music, he farms "'all the interesting things, like sport and shops'" (80). He lives in the cathedral.

Right up to the final chapters, Erskine and Venturus are the enigmas—the only siblings who remain unseen and unheard from. Howard and Awful are able to learn that Erskine farms water, drains, and sewers, that he lives on the outskirts of town in the sewage plant, and that he is, according to Hathaway, "'the only one of us who can really stand up to Archer'" (157). They learn that Venturus is the youngest; that he has brains, like Archer (109); that, according to Torquil, he farms "'all the dull things'" that were left over, like education and housing (80); and that, as his name— "he who is to come"—might suggest, he lives in the future.

Finally, the Goon agrees to take Howard, Awful, and Quentin to see Erskine at the sewage plant. Arriving after a disgusting journey through the sewers at a huge rubbish pit, the three are horrified to discover that Erskine is—the Goon! And Erskine is furious. "'How would *you* like to spend thirty years in a sewer? Know it's been that long. Rest of them think it's thirteen years. *Know* it's been done twice now!'" (175). He has them thrown into a sort of dungeon. But with the help of Ginger, one of Shine's young gang members who has come round to their side, they escape and flee back to town. Howard goes in search of Venturus, who he's now sure must be the one to blame—but where can he find someone who lives in the future?

"'In some house that hasn't been built yet'" (190), suggests Catriona. Remembering that Venturus farms education, Howard tries the unfinished university building; sure enough, as he enters, the building is transformed into a vast temple, and Howard into his own future self.

> He looked at himself with interest in the mirror . . . . Fully grown-up, he seemed to be built on the same huge lines as Erskine, except that—mercifully!—his head was the right size for the rest of him . . . . He wore his hair longish and swept back in a way he did not care for at all. (193)

In one room, Howard finds a heap of typescript on the floor—Quentin's words—in another, an all but finished spaceship being constructed by robots. "Venturus had technology here that made Archer's look like flint axes" (194), he thinks.

Then Erskine shows up. "'You finished now?'" he asks pointedly. "'Or do we go around another thirteen years?'" (197)

The *anagnorisis* hits Howard like "a great Goon fist" in the stomach (197). "I'm Venturus! Howard thought. Oh, no. I can't be! But he knew Erskine was right" (198). With the knowledge, he regains complete memory of his past, and explains everything to his surprisingly sympathetic older brother.

Venturus, the youngest of the seven, was also the most gifted. But "'You all had come into your full powers and could do anything you liked, while I was still just an unprotected child.'" So their parents had laid it on the six older ones not to let Venturus go off on his own. "'It was just the same as me and Awful really. . . . But being our parents, they laid it on you really strong. As long as I was a child, without my powers, you couldn't go away and leave me. I think it was strong enough to come down through Hathaway to Catriona and Quentin. They did adopt me both times'" (199). Later, their parents became disgusted with what their children had grown up to be, and turned them out. The seven settled temporarily in the town and began farming it. But as long as Venturus stayed there, none of the rest could leave. And Venturus did not want to leave till he had finished his spaceship. Space was the final frontier—and so was the sewage farm.

Venturus had to go into the future for the technology to build the ship; he didn't know that living in the future makes you age backwards. When he walked out of the temple after programming his machines, he turned instantly into a baby— and was found by Quentin. "'That was the first time. I didn't realize what had happened until I was thirteen and my powers had started to come back'" (199). Then he remembered, and returned to his spaceship, expecting to find it finished. "'But it wasn't. It was an utter mess. I'd made a mistake in programming the robots'" (200). The thirteen years' work had been wasted.

> "The only thing I could think of to do was to do the same thing all over again . . . . But this time I planned it. I spent a day reprogramming the robots and arranging to pay Quentin and Catriona back for adopting me the first time."
> It had been a frantic day. He remembered how he had

bullied Mountjoy and arranged for Quentin not to pay taxes . . . .

"Just to pay them back?" Erskine asked unbelievingly.

"Well, I thought it might put the rest of you off the scent," Howard-Venturus admitted, "if you thought the words were doing it. But I didn't know they'd adopt me twice. I didn't *know*. I really didn't know that when I went outside and turned into a baby, I was going to take everything back thirteen years with me. I'd no idea!" (200–1).

Now Howard hates being Venturus, and knows that his ambitious siblings must be stopped. The only solution he can see is to send Archer, Dillian, and Shine—the only three who want to farm the world—into space in his beloved spaceship. With Erskine and Torquil, he works out a plan to lure them into the trap. The temple containing the spaceship has to be brought into the present, and all three use their mental powers to pull it, "like pulling a kite out of the sky" (230). Howard is so embarrassed when he sees it from the outside, that he almost lets go again. "Four towering statues of Venturus held up a roof which was a head of Venturus, giant-size, looking heroic and noble and, to Howard's shamed eyes, utterly stupid" (230). The spaceship, needless to say, is named *Venturus* too.

At one point, Archer had given Quentin a new typewriter with a device attached that would actually give words the power to create reality. Quentin had, of course, refused to use it. But now "It pays to increase your word power" [10]. As he types, Archer, Shine, and Dillian do exactly what he is describing, and follow one another into the spaceship. Fifi is allowed to join Archer there, and at the last minute Quentin kindly adds two of Shine's bodyguards to "'make the numbers even'" (237). The spaceship blasts off, and Howard quickly disconnects the special device from the typewriter—just before Quentin can add "And they lived happily ever after."

Erskine plans to travel and see the world, but Howard sees signs that he will be interested in Awful someday. And that worries him a little. He remembers when Awful came to the temple looking for him, and grew older as he watched, turning into "a large, fat schoolgirl . . . with a sudden strong look of Shine" (204).

> Hm, thought Howard. He had been thinking it was his
> duty to stay and help Quentin and Catriona bring Awful
> up, to make up for all the trouble he had caused them.
> They would not want her to be like Shine. Now he saw he
> would have to bring himself up not to be Venturus, too.
> Because it was quite possible that Erskine would come
> back one year, saying he had taken a look at the world and
> decided he would like to farm it. When he did, he would
> offer Awful a share. Howard saw that he and Awful both
> would have to be ready for that day. He thought that since
> this was his third time around, he might just manage to
> get it right for a change. (241)

This, not "They lived happily ever after," is the end of
Archer's Goon.

The speed and suspense of *Archer's Goon* never falter.
Howard, the protagonist, is precipitated into a threatening
situation on the first page, and things keep right on happening—
family crises, chases, battles with Ginger's gang. Yet the main
action is not primarily physical, but mental. At bottom, *Archer's
Goon* resembles the classic mystery story, with a detective
(Howard) who interviews one suspect after another, balancing
contradictory evidence and accumulating pieces of the truth.

The art of these stories is to mislead the reader in such a
way that the *dénouement* is both startling and inevitable—to
make the reader exclaim, "I should have known!" To play fair,
the author must supply the reader with enough clues to solve the
puzzle along with the detective, and must allow the detective no
information which the reader does not have as well.

In *Archer's Goon*, the puzzle is to discover which of the
seven has been getting Quentin's words. It is assumed that
whoever has the words is also responsible for immobilizing the
other six—which is correct, though in an unexpected way. For
the words are, in fact, pure nonsense, just as Quentin had
insisted in the beginning. They are what mystery writers call a
"red herring," a false trail laid to distract the hounds from their
prey. By focusing our attention on Quentin's words and their
supposed power, we let essential clues slip past, unnoticed, and
never realize that Venturus (not to mention Erskine) is under our
noses all along.

The clues are there, when we go back and look for them. One of the strongest is placed cunningly near the beginning. The Goon has carved crude letters into a china mug with his knife, and Quentin ponders them, saying, "'perhaps he tried to carve G for Goon'" and "'It's either a *V* or a *Y* on the other side. Do you think it's *A* for Archer upside down?'" (19). At this point, Archer is the only name of the seven that we know. Near the end, Howard looks at the mug again, and sees at once that the letters are *E* and *V*—Erskine and Venturus. Erskine explains, "'Thought you knew then. Trying to tell you I knew, too'" (228).

Howard's obsession with spaceships and his admiration for Archer and Archer's technology are also clues to his identity. Dillian actually says, "'Spaceships! How interesting! But I suppose you do come under Venturus'" (48). For her, this is simply a connection between Howard's being a schoolboy and Venturus' ties to both education and the future. Howard, whose mind is on the missing words, ignores her remark altogether— the "red herring" technique at work.

Of course, the main reason we don't suspect Howard is that we have been identifying with him and sharing his point of view all the way through the book. Howard is "us"—and we know that we are not supernatural beings. Jones does, however, stress one attribute that Howard has in common with his six giant brothers and sisters, telling us repeatedly that he is big for his age. Hathaway, for example, is described as "almost normal size . . . only a few inches taller than Howard" (149). This implies that Howard, at thirteen, is nearly the size of a full-grown man.

The interview with Hathaway, about two-thirds through, is the point at which the Venturus clues begin to thicken. Hathaway tells Howard that he was adopted; a few pages later, he tells him that Venturus, "'being the youngest, admires Archer almost to the point of worship. He tries to imitate Archer—'" (157). In fact, Hathaway has just realized the truth. Howard senses that Hathaway is "trying to tell him something else, something behind the actual words" (157), but is unable to see the link between Venturus' admiration for Archer and his own. Again, when Hathaway, Dillian, Torquil and Shine all help him escape from Erskine, he experiences "a whole cluster of inklings: If even Shine joined in to help him against Erskine, then—But for some reason, he did not want to think about that" (188). Howard's dislike of his family is so strong that he resists the discovery to the very end. Thus, we can share Howard's thoughts without ever guessing his identity. Mystery fans will remember how Agatha Christie performed a similar feat of prestidigitation in *The Murder of Roger Ackroyd*, in which the first-person narrator turns out to be the murderer.

For the young reader, *Archer's Goon* presents a heady intellectual challenge. Getting those seven siblings straight, checking off the "ten facts," and simply keeping up with what's happening is more than enough without trying to solve the mystery as well. Though none of Howard's "suspects"—unlike those in mystery stories—actually lies to him, none of them knows everything, and all, even Mountjoy, conceal part of what they know. At each successive interview, Howard (and the reader) must process new information, while considering what may have been evaded or left unsaid. The reader shares with Howard an increasing knowledge of the whole picture, and with it that satisfying sense of intellectual mastery associated with E. Nesbit's classic fantasies. At one point, for example, on the trail of Hathaway, Howard consults the school library, "where the second year had set up a project on the town. There was a map, and models, and drawings, and careful pages of history" (138). Knowing that Hathaway lives in the past, Howard searches the map and deduces (correctly) that he can be found in the area marked "Site of Old Abbey." Howard goes off "rather pleased with himself" (139)—yet, ironically, he has just overlooked yet another Venturus clue:

> Someone had even done a drawing of what the new building at the Poly would be like. An Egyptian temple, Howard thought, and he grinned, thinking of Torquil. (138)

"Egyptian," of course, because of the Pharaohnic self-portraits holding up the roof!

The *anagnorisis* comes as a complete shock, to us as well as Howard. What we have been expecting is a climactic confrontation with the elusive Venturus, from which our hero Howard will emerge victorious, having saved his family, his city, and the world. When Howard recognizes the arch-villain as *himself*, the illusion of intellectual mastery is destroyed. Our assumptions about him, about Venturus, about Quentin's words, about what's really happening in *Archer's Goon* go down like a house of cards, and we must turn back to the beginning again with new ones.

Archer's Goon has roots in the E. Nesbit tradition, but its world is the world our children know. Even its magic seems cut off from the past, so intertwined with technology that the book might be classified as science fiction instead of fantasy. The seven brothers and sisters, from whom all the magic emanates, might be powerful extraterrestrial beings, exiled by their parents from some remote star system. Yet the mythical echoes are stronger than those of science fiction; it makes even more sense to think of the seven as beings with divine powers, like the Olympians of Greek mythology. The Olympians, too, had their family spats. They too could take human form, and mate with mortal women, and they too looked on human beings as pawns in their cosmic games. If the Olympians were to reappear in today's world, they would surely divide among themselves not the forces of nature, as they once did, but those sources of power that control our urbanized society—banks, taxation, crime, the police, industry, shopping, transportation, education, electricity, television, and the sewage farm.

Early in the story, Quentin calls them "'seven megalomaniac wizards'" (87), but this is before he and we know how great their powers are; Jones hints in several ways that we are not to regard them as mere human beings who have learned magic, but as something more. They don't age as we do (66), they're bigger than we are, they inhabit huge spaces in separate realms. The youngest of the family is the most powerful, as Zeus was. Venturus actually lives in a temple dedicated to himself, and Torquil in the cathedral. Another hint of godlikeness is dropped when Ginger confides how Shine used mind control to recruit him: "'there was a lot about how marvelous Shine was. Worship Shine'" (181).

As Howard senses his new powers "unfolding inside him," he is startled by the sheer strength of his feelings. "No wonder the whole family just stretched out and took things if they wanted them. Beside those feelings, ordinary people just seemed feeble" (206). Howard, incidentally, is not the first Jones protagonist to be or become a god; she had already explored this audacious possibility in *Drowned Ammet* (1977), *The Spellcoats* (1979), and *Dogsbody*.

Jones had also superimposed a family of gods on the modern world, in *Eight Days of Luke*. Unlike that earlier fantasy, *Archer's Goon* succeeds brilliantly in integrating a mythical realm with our own. A more significant difference between the two works, however, lies in the gods themselves. The gods of Norse mythology are at war with death, cold, and chaos; side by side with the heroes of humanity, they fight to save the universe from destruction. The Olympians have no such moral weight. Their ancient war with the Titans was no struggle of good versus evil; judging by Prometheus, the Titans may well have proved more benevolent to humanity. While David's admiration for Thor and Odin foreshadows a heroic future for him, Howard's admiration for Archer reveals his immaturity and the failings he must overcome.

Drawing on mythical tradition enables Jones, paradoxically, to show us what our world has become. For our world seems to us at once unstable, chaotic, fragmented, and meaningless—yet also bureaucratized, dehumanized, over-controlled. Both extremes deny our value and integrity as individuals, creating a pervasive sense of powerlessness, a vacuum to be filled (for many) by ethnic nationalism or religious fundamentalism or survivalism or Dungeons and Dragons. In *Archer's Goon*, a city has been taken over by gods who control every aspect of human life. Privacy no longer exists; Archer can spy on you through your electric outlets and Erskine through your drains. Published in 1984, *Archer's Goon* deliberately evokes George Orwell's horrifying vision of state control with ARCHER IS WATCHING YOU. At the same time, these gods are working at cross purposes, and their power-political struggles produce increasing chaos. The gods may be all but omnipotent, but they are crazy too.

The "ten facts" at the beginning of the book help create this image of a rigidly controlled yet undependable universe. On the one hand, the book is reduced to a mathematical proof of ten numbered facts. On the other, the facts themselves are nonsensical. As we read *Archer's Goon*, we may attempt to make it "prove" the "facts"; our failure—for of course the book is doing no such thing—reflects the failure of our old rules—our "facts" based on proverbs and cliches—to guide us through a time of unprecedented change. In actuality, the "facts" of *Archer's Goon* were compiled after the book had been written, and inspired by a real-life absurdity. The idea for them came, says Jones,

> from a Dutch research student of my husband's, who told me that all Dutch theses had by law to state in the front ten facts that the thesis was to prove. Most people, he said, ran out of serious facts after three, and usually put things like "Tiggers don't like thistles" for the next seven. This quite enchanted me. ("Letter")

The bizarre world of *Archer's Goon* is our own.

What happens to the Sykeses is only too "realistic." Random power outages, mechanical breakdowns, invasive music, senseless construction projects, budget cuts in school systems, credit and income tax problems are taken for granted in the chaotic bureaucracy we call home. I was interested, but not really surprised, to learn from Diana Wynne Jones herself that

> the remote genesis of the book was when, some years before, the Gas Company dug a ditch round the entire terrace where I live. In order to get out of the house, one had to stand at the gate and shout, whereupon the foreman, an enormous fat bad-tempered man with orange hair—we used to call him Obelix—would come and shout too until one of his minions put down a plank for a bridge over the ditch. ("Letter")

That real-life ditch becomes a powerful image, for the ground beneath our feet is, in the most fundamental sense, our security. Repeatedly in Jones's work, a breach in the earth signals the unleashing of forces that cannot be controlled, all the way back to *The Ogre Downstairs*, when the sown dragons' teeth bring forth savage warriors, sprouting like mushrooms from the parking lot. In *Eight Days of Luke*, David's curse produces an earthquake. "The solid ground came up in ripples under his feet and made him stumble. . . . The top of the wall made a crazy outline against the hot blue sky, wagging up and down, with bricks coming loose and lifting, then banging back into place again, and mortar spurting from between them" (31). Snakes writhe from the heaving ground—and Loki is let loose. Earthquakes and cracking stone warn of impending destruction as Time City "goes critical." In *Archer's Goon*, the seven-foot-wide ditch symbolizes the isolation and destruction threatening the besieged family. It also suggests that nothing, not Earth itself, is safe or secure.

What can we do, when the earth is crumbling beneath our feet? We can still, Jones insists, strive to discern good from evil, and accept our responsibilities. Doing this makes Quentin a hero, if a rather comic one, and Howard a hero in the end. Quentin helps Howard see the truth about Archer, but Howard has to see the truth about Venturus. He has to assume the responsibility he evaded "the last time around" and sacrifice the spaceship that represents his own egotistical desires. Finally, instead of allowing his father to write a happy ending, he has to create his own future. He will "have to bring himself up not to be Venturus," and ensure that he and Awful are both ready if Erskine wants to farm the world someday.

Amid all the questions answered in the climactic section of the story, no one thinks to ask why Howard reacts so differently "this time around." Last time, though grateful enough to Quentin and Catriona to try to repay them through Mountjoy, he was still thinking primarily of what he wanted—his spaceship. This time, he utterly rejects his once and future self, right down to the way Venturus wears his hair (193). He senses the kindness of Hathaway, the sympathy of Erskine, and the loneliness of Torquil. The unabashed egotism of his temple appalls him. He can see how his own arrogance has infected even the design of his spaceship:

> He looked at the console and shook his head sadly. The red foam pilots' couches were about all right, but Venturus had gone mad over the controls. There were banks and banks of unnecessary buttons, levers, and dials. He had been trying to go one better than Archer. And he had. (232)

Howard needs Ginger's help just to push all the buttons down, so that he can program the spaceship to take off and never return to Earth. By the time he has finished, he has "remarkably few regrets" about losing it (232). And he is pleased when Ginger suggests that "'you and me could design a better ship than that'" (233). What has changed him?

The new factor in the equation is his little sister. Awful was not born until the second time around (201). Most only children experience jealousy and anger at the birth of a sibling; one can imagine the gigantic fury of a Venturus forced to share his parents' love. Jones hints at this, when Quentin recalls another time when their power was inexplicably cut off:

> "It was just after Awful was born," he said. "You must remember, Catriona. She kept us awake every night for a month, and I was too busy trying to catch up on sleep to write anything. And quite suddenly, everything in the house was cut off. We'd no light, and no heat, no electricity, no water, and the car wouldn't go either—"
>
> "Yes, I do remember," said Catriona. "Howard screaming as well as Awful, because he was cold, and all the washing." (18–9)

Clearly, Howard himself was to blame; the power failure (and his screams) was simply the unconscious expression of his rage. Yet after this one outburst, he must have grown resigned to his new role. When we first meet him in Chapter One, he has just been defending Awful after school from "twenty angry little girls," and although he dislikes being used as "Awful's secret weapon, . . . he did not feel he could let her down" (2). Being big brother to an obnoxious little sister has cured his egotism, and taught him the unselfishness and responsibility he could have gained no other way.

These are the qualities Howard must have to offset the immense powers he was born with. And power is at the heart of *Archer's Goon*. Archer and his siblings demonstrate the abuse of power, the various forms taken by that abuse, and the need to resist it valiantly, as Quentin does. Howard's temptation to imitate Archer and Awful's to imitate Shine show how dangerously seductive power can be even to a child. Yet without the use of power, society cannot function. "All power corrupts, but we need electricity." Howard must learn not to renounce his powers, but to use them rightly—not to chain the city to his own desires, but to set it free. His last actions in *Archer's Goon* are to remove absolute power from Quentin's reach, and to realize that he must bring up himself and Awful to resist the temptation of absolute power later on.

In a world where people feel powerless as individuals, power is the ultimate temptation, and in the 1980s, greed, selfishness, and the lust for power became the hallmarks of success. *Archer's Goon*, written for the children of the eighties, has a good deal to say about the difficulties of discerning right and wrong in such a world. It does not suggest that the old rules will be much help. It does say something about the kind of person one needs to be, and the responsibility to make oneself that kind of person. In a time of dissolution and destruction, it gives children a place to stand. Now, in the 1990s, we sense change overtaking us once more, unpredictable and inexorable. It will be interesting to see what Diana Wynne Jones writes for the children of the next decade.

Notes

1.   Until E. Nesbit's *Five Children and It* (1902), virtually all fantasy was set in some world other than our own. Sometimes the entire story took place in a world more or less like the world of folktale (for example, *The Princess and the Goblin*); sometimes a child from our own world would enter a magical world where the main part of the story took place (*Alice's Adventures in Wonderland*). E. Nesbit's only significant predecessor was F. Anstey (Thomas Anstey Guthrie), who may well have given her the idea of bringing magic into our world instead. Anstey's famous *Vice Versa*, about a present-day father and son who magically change bodies with each other, was published in 1882— though not as a children's book. His *The Brass Bottle*, whose present-day hero finds himself in possession of a wish-granting genie, was published in 1900, two years before *Five Children and It*, and, like E. Nesbit's fantasy, was first serialized in *The Strand*.

2. Diana Wynne Jones has written an appreciative analysis of Tolkien's structural technique, "The Shape of the Narrative in *The Lord of the Rings*."

3. Ruth Waterhouse provides a close and thoughtful analysis of *Witch Week* in "Which Way to Encode and Decode Fiction?" She too sees Jones's work as strikingly contemporary, suggesting that *Witch Week* draws on theoretical concepts of language and history developed by Saussure and Foucault.

WORKS CITED

Aristotle. *The Rhetoric and the Poetics of Aristotle*. Translated by Ingram Bywater. New York: Modern Library, 1954.

Jones, Diana Wynne. *Archer's Goon*. New York: Greenwillow, 1984.

———. *Charmed Life*. New York: Greenwillow, 1977.

———. *Dogsbody*. New York: Greenwillow, 1977.

———. *Eight Days of Luke*. Harmondsworth: Puffin, 1977.

———. "The Heroic Ideal: A Personal Odyssey." *The Lion and the Unicorn* 13, 1 (1989): 129–40.

———. *The Ogre Downstairs*. New York: Dutton, 1975.

———. Personal letter. 14 May 1991.

———. "The Shape of the Narrative in *The Lord of the Rings*." In *J. R. R. Tolkien: This Far Land*. Ed. by Robert Giddings. London: Vision; Barnes and Noble, 1983. 87–107.

———. *A Tale of Time City*. New York: Greenwillow, 1987.

M.C. Review of *Archer's Goon*. *Junior Bookshelf*, 1984: 264–5.

Nesbit, E. [Edith] *The Story of the Amulet*. Harmondsworth: Puffin, 1959.

Waterhouse, Ruth. "Which Way to Encode and Decode Fiction?" *Children's Literature Association Quarterly* 16, 1 (Spring 1991): 2–6.

Epilogue

Diana Wynne Jones sends seismic quivers through the foundations of fantasy, demanding an inner balance and flexibility of her young readers as well as her characters. Frank Stockton, too, suggested that children not try to "go straight in a crooked house," but accept and adapt to the new and unforeseen that lie in wait for them. Surprisingly, yet somehow reassuringly, the voice of our most contemporary author echoes the author of fairy tales who wrote a hundred years ago, in another time of unsettling change.

Good children's books last. But to stay alive and healthy, a children's book has to be out on the shelves where children can find it. Publishers must believe that they can turn a profit from it; libraries and bookstores must buy it and keep it visible.

Since I began writing the essays which make up this book, several of the long-neglected works I've described have shown signs of renewed vitality. Two substantial paperback collections of Stockton's fairy tales have appeared, as well as an attractive paperback of *Nils* in a more idiomatic translation. A number of Newbery Honor Books long out of print have been resurrected in paperback—among them, *The Moved-Outers*, nearly as topical today as it was fifty years ago. And the sudden flowering of the Betsy-Tacy Society has provided a large and vocal lobby for Maud Hart Lovelace; it seems unlikely that the Betsy-Tacy books will be allowed to go out of print again. Of the other works discussed here, most are currently available, at least in their countries of origin. Even toy theaters are still being manufactured, with their nineteenth-century scripts of *Cinderella*, *Aladdin*, and *Blackbeard the Pirate*.

But being in print is only half the battle. A children's book also needs advocates in the adult sector, not only to keep it on the shelves, but to act as go-betweens—especially if it looks too long, too dull, too odd, too old-fashioned, or too difficult to appeal at first glance. Today's young readers, who do not read as well as they used to, will probably never have the chance to enjoy Stockton's fairy tales or *Nils* or *Island Mackenzie* without adults to read aloud to them.

So it is important for us to know about books like these, to appreciate what is uniquely valuable about each of them, and to share what we rediscover. The "realms of gold" are richer than they ever were, but much of it is hidden treasure. We should not rest content until we have it all.

Index